Making Headway
Advanced

Literature

Bill Bowler
Sue Parminter

Oxford University Press 1992

Oxford University Press
Walton Street, Oxford OX2 6DP

Oxford New York Toronto Madrid
Delhi Bombay Calcutta Madras Karachi
Kuala Lumpur Singapore Hong Kong Tokyo
Nairobi Dar es Salaam Cape Town
Melbourne Auckland

and associated companies in
Berlin Ibadan

OXFORD and OXFORD ENGLISH are trade marks of
Oxford University Press

ISBN 0 19 435 5063
© Oxford University Press 1992

Phototypeset by Tradespools Ltd, Frome,
Somerset

Printed by Interprint Limited, Malta

Acknowledgements

The authors and publishers would like to thank the
following for their kind permission to use copyright material.
We apologize for those instances where we have been
unable to trace the copyright holder before printing. If
notified, the publisher will be pleased to rectify any error or
omission at the earliest opportunity.

Boy by Roald Dahl. Publishers Jonathan Cape Ltd. and
Penguin Books Ltd.

'Resolution' by Audrey Longbottom, taken from *Relatives
and Reliques*, published by Transpareon Press.

'The Adventure of Johnnie Waverly', by Agatha Christie,
taken from *Poirot's Early Cases*. Copyright © Agatha Christie
Ltd. 1974.

'Matilda' by Hilaire Belloc, from *The Complete Verse of Hilaire
Belloc*, reprinted by permission of the Peter Fraser and
Dunlop Group Ltd.

Softcops and Fen by Caryl Churchill. Published by Methuen
Drama.

An Artist of the Floating World by Kazuo Ishiguro. Published
by Faber & Faber Ltd.

'The River God' by Stevie Smith, from *Collected Poems of
Stevie Smith* (Penguin 20th Century Classics). James
MacGibbon, Executor. For the USA reprinted by permission
of New Directions Publishing Corporation.

'Building for the Future' by Anne Turner from *Scottish Short
Stories* 1977. HarperCollins Publishers Ltd.

'What were they like?' by Denise Levertov. Copyright ©
1971 by Denise Levertov Goodman. Reprinted by permission
of New Directions Publishing Corporation.

'Old Man of the Temple' by R K Narayan, taken from *Under
the Banyan Tree*, published by William Heinemann Ltd. and
Penguin Books Ltd. Reprinted by permission of Sheil Land
Associates Ltd., Literary Agents.

'Innocent's Song' by Charles Causley, taken from *Collected
Poems*, published by Macmillan.

Authors' Acknowledgements

The authors would like to acknowledge their indebtedness to
the following works dealing with the exploitation of literary
texts in the language classroom, and the exploration of
language use in the literature classroom:

Literature and Language Teaching (ed Christopher Brumfit and
Ronald Carter, OUP); *Literature in the Language Classroom* by
Joanne Collie and Stephen Slater (CUP); *Reading, Analysing &
Teaching Literature* (ed Mick Short, Longman); *Teaching
Literature* by Ronald Carter and Michael N. Long (Longman);
Stylistics and the Teaching of Literature by H G Widdowson
(Longman); *Literature* by Alan Duff and Alan Maley (OUP).

In addition we would like to thank everyone at Oxford
University Press for their part in the shaping of this book.
Finally, we would like to thank John and Liz Soars for their
careful reading of the manuscript, their invaluable criticism,
and their inspiring advice.

Illustrations by:

Jenny Brackley
David Nicholls
Technical Graphics Department OUP

The publishers would like to thank the following for
permission to reproduce photographs:

Barnaby's Picture Library
Bodleian Library, Oxford
Bridgeman Art Library
Camera Press/Jane Bowin
Edifice/Darcey
William Heinemann Ltd.
Hulton Picture Library/Deutsch Collection
Shakespeare Centre
Mary Evans Picture Library
James MacGibbon
New Directions Publishing Corporation/David Geier
Ronald Grant Collection
Mark Gerson

Contents

Foreword

Literature

For hundreds of years, the role of literature in the foreign language curriculum was unquestioned. It was believed that learners could only appreciate a language through the study of its highest form of expression. Literature was seen as the only way to get to know a nation's culture, and in many cases, its people. Even though the literary language was often above the level of the learner, and the vocabulary load unbearable, classes persevered in their laborious word-by-word translation of entire books.

Times changed. The 1970s and 80s saw teachers striving to bring the outside world into their classrooms, and the clarion call was for authentic material such as train timetables and newspaper extracts to help learners to cope with the real world. Literature was not so much ousted as put into a corner and forgotten. There was even some question as to whether literature could be considered authentic or not!

Perhaps we have now achieved a more reasonable balance. Literature can be taught in an interesting and eye-opening way. Later-level students are ready to read longer texts and whole books, and they appreciate passages with more substance and diversity than can be provided by a daily newspaper.

This book will serve as excellent source material for teachers. The authors have selected a wide range of texts from prose, drama, and poetry from different centuries. Some texts will amuse, others will be thought-provoking, but all will provide a challenge and a topic for discussion. Students are led into the texts via pre-comprehension tasks, and the texts are exploited via language and skills-based exercises. Personalization runs throughout.

It would be most rewarding if students were inspired to read the original books after having been introduced to them through extracts in *Literature*. We feel sure they will do so!

John and Liz Soars
Series editors

Introduction

Who this book is for

Students This book is for students at advanced level who would like to start reading some literature in English. It is ideal for class work or for students working independently.

Teachers This book is for teachers who would like to introduce their students to the pleasures of reading literature in English. The book is divided into thematic units, some of which explore topics and issues raised in *Headway Advanced*. It can, however, be used on its own or to supplement any advanced course.

What the book contains

It is a collection of literary texts and accompanying exercises designed to provide enjoyment, vocabulary enrichment, and reading skills development. We hope that *Literature* will encourage advanced students to explore more literature in English on their own, as well as help them to develop the skills they need to do so.

It is not a course in English literature, although poetry, prose, and drama by famous authors such as Shakespeare, Charlotte Brontë, and Oscar Wilde are included, as well as contemporary works by familiar and less well-known authors.

The book focuses mainly on British writers, but it also features works in English by writers of different nationalities.

How the book is organized

Each of the fourteen units takes approximately one and a half hours of class time. The main focus of each unit is a literary text.

Each unit:
- starts with biographical information about the author.
- provides support for students and teachers by systematically dealing with important new vocabulary items in the text.
- contains varied and stimulating comprehension and text interpretation activities.

Each unit is organized in three steps:
Before reading → preparing for the text
While reading → exploring the meaning of the text
After reading → responding imaginatively to the text

The book is accompanied by an audio tape with readings of all the texts. Sometimes the taped material is essential to an exercise, sometimes students are encouraged to listen to it as they read, or after they have finished reading, simply to enhance their enjoyment and reinforce their comprehension of the text.

The answer key at the end of the book helps the teacher and allows the students to use the book independently. Cultural information necessary for a full appreciation of the texts appears either in footnotes or in the answer key.

How to use the book

To the teacher

1 Although you can dip into the book at any point, the easier texts and activities are at the beginning, and the more challenging ones at the end.

2 If you want to cut down on class time per unit, you could set the pre-text vocabulary activity as preparatory homework.

3 Some of the texts included in *Literature* have been made into films. Watching a video is a rewarding way for students to get a better understanding of the complete story. In a monolingual class, a subtitled version of the film can be useful.

4 Some additional tasks that students can try outside class are:
   – comparing an original literary text in English with a translation in their mother tongue.
   – reading a longer literary text first in their mother tongue before looking at key passages in English.

To the student

1 We recommend that you use a good English/English dictionary while you work through the vocabulary exercises.

2 The words you meet in the vocabulary exercises are those you need to know before you read the texts. The vocabulary exercises do not deal with all the possible meanings, or even the most common meaning of these words, but with their specific meaning in the literary text which follows. We do not suggest that you try to learn all these words.

3 Be careful not to use a dictionary all the time as you read. The essential vocabulary is dealt with in the pre-text exercises. Try to guess the meaning of new words from the context, or to ignore unknown words the first time you read a text.

4 If you are using this book on your own, try to find someone else to work through the discussion activities with.

Introductory unit

What is literature?

Which of the following would you classify as literature? (Check any new words in a dictionary.)

Shakespeare	Play scripts	Nursery rhymes
Novels	Comic verse	Short stories
Modern poetry	Autobiographies	Song lyrics
Science fiction	Comic strips	Fairy stories
Film scripts	Oscar Wilde	Horror stories
Agatha Christie	Ballads	Travel writing

Why study literature in English language classes?

Which of the following students' statements do you agree with? Compare your response with the responses of other students. What do *you* think about studying literature in English language classes?

1 'Reading poetry aloud has helped me with my pronunciation, especially rhythm and stress. Reading prose aloud has helped to make my intonation more fluent and natural.'

2 'Studying short stories and poems in English is great. It's good to find you can understand something that's written for native English speakers to read, instead of something specially written for language students.'

3 'I don't read literature in my own language, so why should I read it in English?'

4 'Studying novels and short stories in English gives you lots of cultural information about English-speaking countries which you can't find in most English language coursebooks.'

5 'After reading a poem there are usually lots of things to discuss. Even when you understand the literal meaning of all the words, you often have to "read between the lines" to understand the deeper message.'

6 'Plays, novels, and short stories often use lots of colourful idioms and expressions. It's very interesting to look at different styles of writing.'

7 'Literature is full of old-fashioned and poetic words. I don't want to speak

like a book. I want to learn up-to-date, everyday, modern English that I can use in real-life situations.'

8 'I think studying literary texts is a good way to learn or revise vocabulary. The language of a poem stays in my mind longer than the words from the page of a coursebook.'

9 'In my opinion, English writers such as Shakespeare employ superior English when compared to ordinary folk in this day and age. It is for this very reason that I dearly love studying literature.'

Vocabulary of literature

1 Put the following words into the correct columns below. Some words may fit into more than one column. Use your dictionary to check the meaning and the pronunciation of any new words.

anthology	author	chapter	character
comedy	description	dialogue	dramatist
essayist	fiction	narration	non-fiction
novelist	paragraph	playwright	plot
poet	point of view	pseudonym	rhyme
scene	script	setting	stage directions
stanza	tragedy	verse	whodunnit

Prose	Poetry	Drama

2   Read the following sentences. (Don't use a dictionary!)

a.   There's a picture of a heart at the end of this sentence.

b.   Sentence a. is literally true.

c.   My heart broke when she left me.

d.   Sentence c. is figurative. My heart didn't *really* break. The literal meaning is 'I was very sad'.

e.   There is a picture of a visage /'vɪzɪdʒ/ at the end of this sentence.

f.   The seventh word in sentence e. is archaic. We don't normally use words like this nowadays, though they were common in past centuries. (The twenty-eighth word in i. is the modern equivalent.)

g.   'My love is like a red, red rose.' *Robert Burns (1759–1796)*

h.   The rose in sentence g. is an image of the Scottish poet Robert Burns' love. He is saying that the woman he loves is exactly like a rose.

i.   The last sentence above is false. The woman may be beautiful and fresh, like a rose, but only certain things in the image are like her. Her face isn't bright red, she isn't a plant, she hasn't got a green stalk, or sharp thorns.

j.   Poppies are bright red flowers which grow in fields. They only last for a short time before they die.

k.   'In Flanders fields the poppies blow
Between the crosses, row on row . . .'

l.   The two lines in k. come from a poem about World War I by the Canadian poet John McCrae (1872–1918).

m.   The poppies in k. symbolize the British and allied soldiers who died fighting in Flanders during the War.

3   Now translate the following words into your language:

figurative /'fɪgərətɪv/ _____

literal /'lɪtərəl/ _____

image /'ɪmɪdʒ/ _____

archaic /ɑːˈkeɪɪk/ _____

symbolize /'sɪmbəlaɪz/ _____

1 Trouble at school

ROALD DAHL *was born in 1916. He became famous as a children's writer with books such as* Charlie and the Chocolate Factory *and* Revolting Rhymes, *and for his strange 'sting-in-the-tail' short stories and novels for adults. He was born in Wales although his parents were Norwegian. He travelled a great deal before he started writing, and lived in London, Dar-es-Salaam, Greece, Syria, and the United States. In 1942 he went to Washington as a diplomat, and it was there that he began writing short stories. His book* Boy *was first published in 1984. He died in 1990.*

What do you think?

Oscar Wilde

Agatha Christie

Hilaire Belloc

Charlotte Brontë

William Shakespeare

Stevie Smith

- How many of these writers do you know?
- What do you know about them?
- Are you interested in personal details about writers you like?
- Which writers would you like to know more about?
- Do you like reading biographies and autobiographies?
- When you read a biography or an autobiography what kind of information do you find most interesting?

Vocabulary

Match a word in **A** with a definition in **B**.

A	B
1 form (*noun*)	a. to shout loudly, often in anger or pain
2 mutter (*verb*)	b. to stay in one place
3 hideous (*adjective*)	c. to speak with difficulty, hesitating at the beginning of words
4 yell (*verb*)	d. very ugly
5 stutter (*verb*)	e. a school class
6 flick (*verb*)	f. clever at deceiving people
7 settle (*verb*)	g. to produce a gentle, unsteady light
8 sly (*adjective*)	h. to push into something violently, usually with a pointed object
9 glimmer (*verb*)	i. to speak very quietly, usually complaining
10 venom (*noun*)	j. a feeling of bitterness and hatred
11 stab (*verb*)	k. to move with a short, sudden movement

Reading

The following passage is from *Boy* by Roald Dahl. It is about childhood and school experiences.

Read the extract and decide which of the following titles best summarizes it. Give reasons for your choice.

1 Crime	4 Innocence
2 Punishment	5 Guilt
3 Capture	6 Repentance

EVERY BOY in our form was watching Mr Coombes and Mrs Pratchett as they came walking down the line towards us.

'Nasty cheeky lot, these little 'uns!' I heard Mrs Pratchett muttering. 'They comes into my shop and they thinks they can do what they damn well likes!' 5

Mr Coombes made no reply to this.

'They nick things when I ain't lookin',' she went on. 'They put their grubby 'ands all over everything and they've got no manners. I don't mind girls. I never 'ave no trouble with girls, but boys is 'ideous and 'orrible! I don't 'ave to tell *you* that, 'Eadmaster, do I?' 10

'These are the smaller ones,' Mr Coombes said.

I could see Mrs Pratchett's piggy little eyes staring hard at the face of each boy she passed.

Suddenly she let out a high-pitched yell and pointed a dirty finger straight at Thwaites. 'That's 'im!' she yelled. 'That's one of 'em! I'd know 15 'im a mile away, the scummy little bounder!'

The entire school turned to look at Thwaites. 'W-what have *I* done?' he stuttered, appealing to Mr Coombes.

'Shut up,' Mr Coombes said.

Mrs Pratchett's eyes flicked over and settled on my own face. I looked *20* down and studied the black asphalt surface of the playground.

''Ere's another of 'em!' I heard her yelling. 'That one there!' She was pointing at me now.

'You're quite sure?' Mr Coombes said.

'Of course I'm sure!' she cried. 'I never forgets a face, least of all when it's *25* as sly as that! 'Ee's one of 'em all right! There was five altogether! Now where's them other three?'

The other three, as I knew very well, were coming up next.

Mrs Pratchett's face was glimmering with venom as her eyes travelled beyond me down the line. *30*

'There they are!' she cried out, stabbing the air with her finger. ''Im . . . and 'im . . . and 'im! That's the five of 'em all right! We don't need to look no farther than this, 'Eadmaster! They're all 'ere, the nasty dirty little pigs! You've got their names, 'ave you?'

'I've got their names, Mrs Pratchett,' Mr Coombes told her. 'I'm much *35* obliged to you.'

'And I'm much obliged to *you*, 'Eadmaster,' she answered.

As Mr Coombes led her away across the playground, we heard her saying, 'Right in the jar of Gobstoppers* it was! A stinkin' dead mouse which I will never forget as long as I live!' *40*

*Gobstoppers – large, round, brightly-coloured sweets

Comprehension check

Here are some questions about the passage. You can't answer all of them. First, read the passage again. Then, work with a partner. Cross out all the questions you can't answer and answer the questions you don't cross out. Give reasons for your answers.

1 Who is Mr Coombes?
2 Who is Mrs Pratchett?
3 Who is Thwaites?
4 Who is the narrator?
5 What kind of shop does Mrs Pratchett have?
6 Do Mr Coombes and Mrs Pratchett like each other?
7 How old is the narrator in the story?
8 What did the narrator and his four friends do?
9 Why did Mr Coombes take the boys' names?
10 What is going to happen to the boys?
11 What does Mrs Pratchett look like?
12 Where does the scene take place?
13 When does the scene take place?
14 What kind of school is it?
15 Why are all the boys lined up?

> If you would like to know the answers to the rest of the questions or if you like the extract, you could read *Boy* by Roald Dahl.

Listening

T.1

Listen to the passage as you read it again.

Points of style

1 General structure

a. What do you notice about Mrs Pratchett's grammar and pronunciation?
b. What does the way she speaks tell you about Mrs Pratchett?
c. Look at the direct speech in the passage. What does the author achieve by using direct instead of reported speech?
d. Is the sentence structure of the passage as a whole simple or complex? Why is it like this?

2 Slang vocabulary

a. Mrs Pratchett uses a number of slang words and expressions. Read the passage again, and underline the words and expressions that you think are slang. Work in pairs. Compare the words you have underlined. Are they the same?

b. Find the slang equivalents in the passage for the words below. They are in the same order as the words appear in the text.

1	unpleasant	4	dirty (×2)
2	rude and disrespectful	5	a rascal
3	to steal	6	smelly

Discussion and roleplay

Step one

The class should divide into three groups. In your groups, add to the list of possible school punishments below.

– Corporal punishment
– Writing lines
– Detention (staying late after school)

Step two

Stay in your groups. Decide on a letter (A, B, or C) for your group, as follows:

Group A   You are headteachers.
Group B   You are form teachers.
Group C   You are parents.

In your character group, discuss the two school punishment cases below. Read the cases and agree on the following:

- why the children did what they did
- how serious the offence is
- how they can be stopped from repeating the offence
- an appropriate punishment

PUNISHMENT CASE 1 – *Tommy Traddles*   Tommy is 10. He is an average student. He was caught cheating in some exams. These exams are important because the result decides what type of secondary school he will go to. Tommy's father has just left his mother.

PUNISHMENT CASE 2 – *Sandra Griffin*   Sandra is 16. She is a bright student but often in trouble for her behaviour. She was absent all last week. On Monday she arrived at school with a note from her mother explaining that she had been ill. The headteacher discovered that Sandra had written the note. Sandra had gone away to London with a group of friends. She had told her parents that she was going away on a Biology field trip.

Step three

Now divide into groups of three, with one A student, one B student, and one C student in each group. Discuss both of the punishment cases, and decide on a punishment. You must reach a group decision in each case.

Compare your solutions with the other groups in the class.

2 A housewife speaks

AUDREY LONGBOTTOM *is a contemporary Australian poet. She comes from New South Wales. Her poems and stories have been published in many Australian journals. 'Resolution' comes from her book* Relatives *and* Reliques, *published in 1979. It was commended in the Commonwealth Poetry Prize Competition of 1980.*

Discussion

Think of your household in the morning.

– Who gets up first?
– Who makes the breakfast? What does everyone else do?
– Do you have any pets? What do they do in the morning?
– Does anything ever go wrong? What?

Vocabulary

Look at the following sentences. Don't use a dictionary. Try to guess the meaning of the underlined words.

Example
Lavender looks nice in the garden, and it smells nice too.
Lavender is a noun. Perhaps it's a flower or a plant.

1 Last New Year's Eve I made a resolution to give up smoking.

2 He took his gun, aimed it carefully, and shot the tiger through the head.

3 His girlfriend was very angry when he arrived late. He placated her by buying her flowers and inviting her to lunch.

4 When a fish bites a fish hook it can't easily escape. This is because the little metal barbs on the hook stick in the fish's mouth.

5 The dentist couldn't repair my bad tooth, so she extracted it.

6 The President said with great dignity that his country was small, but that his people were honest and hard-working.

7 This soup is too salty! You can't give muck like this to our customers!

8 Calling someone a pig is a strong <u>insult</u> in some languages.

9 King Richard I of England <u>earned</u> the name 'Richard the Lionheart' because of his great courage.

Look up the unknown words in a dictionary. Check how close your guesses are to the dictionary definitions.

Reading 1

Look at the following text.
- Who is it by?
- What is it about?
- What mood or atmosphere does it create?

Resolution:

Tomorrow will be different. I'll get up early, organize the children, send them neatly to school, my husband quietly to work, and I shall surprise with gentleness: eyes lowered, dressed in blue, smelling of lavender, hair parted in the middle.

    Shouting is over, and the little monsters gone hot-eyed to school after   5
placating the cat, kicked only beyond its dignity; and him, at work, no doubt extracting the barbs of insults well-earned and aimed. Now I shall clear away the muck of this half-eaten breakfast, then get dressed, and by tonight it will be all right, and tomorrow will be different.

Comprehension check

1 What does the woman usually do in the morning?

2 How are her children usually dressed when they go to school? In what sort of mood does her husband usually go to work?

3 Is the description of the woman in lines 3–4 a realistic picture of a housewife?

4 Did the children kick the cat hard enough to injure it? What did they do afterwards before they went off to school? (lines 5–6)

5 Who earned the insults? Who aimed them? Why are the insults described as having barbs? (lines 6–7)

6 Will everything really be all right by tonight, do you think? Will tomorrow really be different?

Reading 2

Now look at the same text arranged as a poem.

1 Does the layout on the page make a difference to your understanding of the text?

2 Can you see hair? A waist? A skirt?

3 What else can you see in the shape? Are the capital letters important?

$$R^E S^O {}^{LU}T_{I}{}_O{}_N$$

Tomorrow
will be
different
I'll get up early
$$o_r{}_{g}{}_{an}{}^{.z}{}^{i}e\ the\ c_{h.}{}^{n}{}^{e}{}_{ld}{}^{r}{}_{i}$$
send them neatly to school
my husband quietly to work
and I shall surprise
with gentleness eyes
$$l\quad\quad d\atop o\ {}_{wer}\ e$$
dressed in blue
smelling of lavender
hair parted in the
$$m^i{}^{dd}{}_l e$$

SHOUTING IS OVER AND
the little monsters gone
hot-eyed to school after
placating the cat kicked only
beyond its dignity and him at
work no doubt extracting the barbs
of insults well earned and aimed
now I shall clear away the muck of this
half eaten breakfast then get dressed
and by tonight it will be all right and
Tomorrow
will be
different

5

10

15

20

25

Listening and reading aloud

| T.2 |

Listen to the poem. Do you like it better read aloud or written on the page? Why?

Now work in pairs. Take turns reading the poem aloud.

Writing

Write about the same situation that Audrey Longbottom describes from the point of view of the husband, one of the children, the cat, or a neighbour. You can write either a poem or a piece of prose.

Example
(The husband's point of view)

*My wife and I used to be
happy together,
but now
we tear each other to pieces
with sharp words . . .*

(The older child's point of view)

My mum always shouts at us in the morning. She hits me and my sister round the head if we don't behave . . .

3 Whodunnit

AGATHA CHRISTIE *was born in Britain in 1890. She is well known all over the world as the Queen of Crime. She wrote 77 detective novels and books of stories, which have been translated into many languages. She began writing detective fiction at the end of the First World War when she created Hercule Poirot, the little Belgian detective. Her other world-famous creation is Miss Marple, whom many readers identify with Agatha Christie herself. She died in 1976. 'The Adventure of Johnnie Waverly' comes from* Poirot's Early Cases, *a collection of her short stories first published in 1974.*

Reading

A = Tredwell   B = Miss Collins   C = Inspector McNeil   D = Mr Waverley
E = Johnny Waverley

Look at the picture of a scene from a detective story. In the story, a Belgian detective, Hercule Poirot /ˈɜːkjuːl ˈpwɑːrəʊ/ investigates the case of a kidnapped child, Johnnie Waverly.

Mr and Mrs Waverly were warned in an anonymous letter that their son would be kidnapped on the twenty-ninth of the month at exactly twelve o'clock. In the extract below Mr Waverly meets Hercule Poirot some days later and tells him the story of the kidnapping.

The picture on page 19 shows what was happening at exactly twelve o'clock, but there are a number of mistakes in it. Read the extract and, on the picture, circle the differences between what you can see and what you read.

'INSPECTOR McNeil arrived about ten-thirty. The servants had all left by then. He declared himself quite satisfied with the internal arrangements. He had various men posted in the park outside, guarding all the approaches to the house, and he assured me that if the whole thing were not a hoax, we should undoubtedly catch my mysterious correspondent.   5

'I had Johnnie with me, and he and I and the inspector went together into a room we call the council chamber. The inspector locked the door. There is a big grandfather clock there, and as the hands drew near to twelve I don't mind confessing that I was as nervous as a cat. There was a whirring sound, and the clock began to strike. I clutched at Johnnie. I had a feeling a   10
man might drop from the skies. The last stroke sounded, and as it did so, there was a great commotion outside – shouting and running. The inspector flung up the window, and a constable came running up.

'"We've got him sir," he panted. "He was sneaking up through the bushes. He's got a whole dope outfit on him."   15

'We hurried out on the terrace where two constables were holding a ruffianly-looking fellow in shabby clothes, who was twisting and turning in a vain endeavour to escape. One of the policemen held out an unrolled parcel which they had wrested from their captive. It contained a pad of cotton wool and a bottle of chloroform. It made my blood boil to see it. There was   20
a note, too, addressed to me. I tore it open. It bore the following words: "You should have paid up. To ransom your son will now cost you fifty thousand. In spite of all your precautions he has been abducted on the twenty-ninth as I said."

'I gave a great laugh, the laugh of relief, but as I did so I heard the hum of   25
a motor and a shout. I turned my head. Racing down the drive towards the south lodge at a furious speed was a low, long grey car. It was the man who drove it who shouted, but that was not what gave me a shock of horror. It was the sight of Johnnie's flaxen* curls. The child was in the car beside him.

'The inspector ripped out an oath. "The child was here not a minute   30
ago," he cried. His eyes swept over us. We were all there: myself, Tredwell, Miss Collins. "When did you last see him, Mr Waverly?"

'I cast my mind back, trying to remember. When the constable had called us, I had run out with the inspector, forgetting all about Johnnie.

'And then there came a sound that startled us, the chiming of a church   35
clock from the village. With an exclamation the inspector pulled out his watch. It was exactly twelve o'clock. With one common accord we ran to the council chamber; the clock there marked the hour as ten minutes past.

*flaxen – fair

Someone must have deliberately tampered with it, for I have never known
it gain or lose before. It is a perfect timekeeper.'   40
 Mr Waverly paused. Poirot smiled to himself and straightened a little mat
which the anxious father had pushed askew.
 'A pleasing little problem, obscure and charming,' murmured Poirot. 'I
will investigate it for you with pleasure. Truly it was planned *à merveille**.'
 Mrs Waverly looked at him reproachfully. 'But my boy,' she wailed.   45

*à merveille /æ'meəveɪ/ – a
French phrase meaning
'marvellously'

🔑—0

Comprehension check

1 Make sentences which correspond to the text by matching a line in **A** with
one in **B**, and another in **C**. (You can use each line only once.)

A	B	C
a. Johnnie	was interested in	in a car
b. Poirot	forgot to take	10 minutes
c. The constable	was in charge of	Johnnie outside
d. The man	was worried about	the case
e. Inspector McNeil	was driven away	Johnnie
f. Mrs Waverly	intended to	the case
g. Mr Waverly	had been put forward	drug and kidnap Johnnie
h. A note	caught	on the man
i. The grandfather clock	was found	a man

T.3

🔑—0

2 Write out the complete sentences. Listen and put the sentences in the order
in which the facts are mentioned.

_____

_____

_____

_____

_____

_____

_____

_____

_____

_____

Vocabulary

Find the words below in the text. Tick (✓) the meaning which best matches the meaning of each word as it is used in the text.

1 to post (line 3)
   a. to make someone stand
       somewhere ✓
   b. to send to someone
   c. to stand straight as a post

2 a hoax (line 5)
   a. the truth
   b. a trick
   c. an argument

3 a correspondent (line 5)
   a. someone who writes letters
   b. someone who looks like
       someone else
   c. a reporter

4 to clutch (line 10)
   a. to hold tightly
   b. to hit
   c. to smile

5 a commotion (line 12)
   a. a gardener
   b. a storm
   c. a lot of noise

6 to fling up (line 13)
   a. to open slowly
   b. to break
   c. to open hurriedly and
       forcefully

7 to sneak up (line 14)
   a. to move quickly and noisily
   b. to look carefully
   c. to approach secretly

8 shabby (line 17)
   a. in bad condition
   b. clean and new
   c. brightly coloured

9 a vain endeavour (line 18)
   a. a successful attempt
   b. a hopeless attempt
   c. a hopeless wish

10 to ransom (line 22)
   a. to find something
   b. to take away
   c. to pay for someone's
       freedom

11 to abduct (line 23)
   a. to hide a person or thing
   b. to kill someone
   c. to take someone away by
       force

12 to tamper with (line 39)
   a. to change by mistake
   b. to change something you
       shouldn't
   c. to wind up

13 anxious (line 42)
   a. guilty
   b. carefree
   c. worried

14 askew (line 42)
   a. not straight
   b. tidy
   c. upside down

15 to wail (line 45)
   a. to shout with anger
   b. to cry with sadness
   c. to speak very quickly

What do you think?

Which of the following do you think are true? Give reasons for your answers.

1 The Waverlys are very rich.
2 Johnnie is quite young.
3 Poirot solves the crime.
4 Inspector McNeil solves the crime.
5 Mr Waverly is lying.
6 Tredwell wasn't involved in the kidnapping.
7 The man in the garden knows nothing about the kidnapping.
8 Mrs Waverly was ill at the time that Johnnie was kidnapped.
9 The man in the garden changed the time on the clock.
10 The boy in the car was Johnnie.
11 Johnnie was kidnapped by his father.

> To find out if your predictions are correct, you should either read the short story by Agatha Christie called 'The Adventure of Johnnie Waverly', or look in the key at the back of the book.

Writing

Write an article for a newspaper reporting the kidnapping. Use one of the headlines and first lines below to start your report.

WAVERLY HEIR KIDNAPPED

The only son of millionaire couple Mr and Mrs Marcus Waverly was kidnapped yesterday afternoon in a daring raid on Waverly Court, the family home in Surrey.

CLOCK KIDNAP MYSTERY

A vital clue in the Johnnie Waverly kidnapping case is the family grandfather clock, which was mysteriously tampered with yesterday, shortly before the three-year-old disappeared.

£50,000 Ransom in Kidnap Case

Kidnappers have demanded a £50,000 ransom for the release of three-year-old Johnnie Waverly, who was snatched from his parents' home in Surrey yesterday.

4 Never tell a lie

HILAIRE BELLOC *was born in France in 1870. He was brought up in France and England and educated at Oxford. Although both French and Irish blood ran in his veins, he is said by his friends to have been a true Englishman. From 1906 to 1910 he was a Liberal MP, and in World War I he worked as a driver in the French Army. He wrote a great many books of poetry and essays, as well as several novels, and travel and history books. Sadly, he never made much money from his writing while he lived. He is best remembered for his* Cautionary Tales, *which were first published in 1907. He died in 1953.*

Discussion

Discuss these questions in groups.

– Many traditional stories for children contain a moral, or message. Do you remember any stories like this that you were told as a child? What effect did they have on you?

– Do you/Would you read stories with morals to your children? Why/Why not? Do you think children's stories on audio or video cassettes are a good idea?

Vocabulary

1 Word building
Look at the sentences below. The words in brackets at the end of each sentence can be used to make a word that fits in the gap. Use a dictionary to help you.

a. Although she was bored by all the after-dinner speeches, she sat smiling throughout the whole *proceeding*. (proceed)

b. Rheumatism is a family _____ . My grandmother had it, my mother has it, and I expect I'll get it too. (infirm)

c. There was a very _____ programme on the radio last night – all about foreigners' attitudes to Britain. (entertain)

d. Her childhood, spent with her brothers and sisters in a Harlem slum, was a time of great _____ . (deprive)

e. A British team yesterday _____ in climbing Mount Everest by the difficult northern route. (success)

f. She took me into her _____ and told me that her boyfriend had just left her. (confide)

g. He's a _____ child. He never says 'please' or 'thank you'! (dread)

2 Synonyms

~~summoned~~	noble	gallant	aid	peculiar
souse	pains	bawl	band	just

Find a synonym in the box above for each word in brackets below. Use a dictionary to help you.

a. The queen (called) _summoned_ her ministers to advise her.

b. They make a tasty fish soup which is (special) _____ to that part of the country.

c. We were unable to offer any (help) _____ .

d. He looked very (aristocratic) _____ in his officer's uniform.

e. I don't like children who (cry) _____ all the time.

f. King Solomon was a (fair) _____ man.

g. She was waiting for a (heroic) _____ knight to come along and rescue her from the dragon.

h. He was the leader of a (group) _____ of robbers living in the forest.

i. She took great (trouble) _____ to buy the kind of cigars he liked.

j. 'Don't (soak) _____ the salad in vinegar! You know I don't like it,' he said self-importantly.

Listening

1 The pictures on page 26 are illustrations from a poem which tells the story of a girl called Matilda. The poem, also called 'Matilda', is by Hilaire Belloc.

The pictures are in the order they come in the poem. Use them to guess the story.

T.4   Now listen to the poem to see if your guesses are correct.

2   Each pair of lines in the poem rhymes.

Sometimes the rhymes are exact: Lies/Eyes (lines 1–2).

At other times the words are forced to rhyme: Matilda/killed her (lines 5–6).

Try to fill the gaps in the poem using the rhymes, and what you remember of the poem, to help you. (Do not listen to the tape again!)

MATILDA

Matilda told such Dreadful Lies,
It made one Gasp and Stretch one's Eyes;
Her Aunt, who, from her Earliest _____,
Had kept a Strict Regard for Truth,
Attempted to Believe Matilda: 5
The effort very nearly killed her,
And would have done so, had not She
Discovered this Infirmity.
For once, towards the Close of Day,
Matilda, growing tired of _____,   10
And finding she was left alone,
Went tiptoe to the _____
And summoned the Immediate Aid
of London's Noble _____.
Within an hour the Gallant Band   15
Were pouring in on every hand,
From Putney, Hackney Downs and Bow*,
With Courage high and Hearts a-glow
They galloped, roaring through the _____,
'Matilda's House is Burning Down!'   20
Inspired by British Cheers and Loud
Proceeding from the Frenzied Crowd,
They ran their ladders through a score
Of windows on the Ball Room _____;
And took Peculiar Pains to Souse   25
The Pictures up and down the _____,
Until Matilda's Aunt succeeded
In showing them they were not _____
And even then she had to _____
To get the Men to go away!   30

It happened that a few Weeks _____
Her Aunt was off to the Theatre
To see that Interesting _____
The Second Mrs Tanqueray.†
She had refused to take her _____   35
To hear this Entertaining Piece:
A Deprivation Just and Wise
To Punish her for Telling _____
That Night a Fire *did* break _____ –
You should have heard Matilda Shout!   40
You should have heard her Scream and Bawl,
And throw the window up and _____
To People passing in the _____ –
(The rapidly increasing Heat
Encouraging her to obtain   45
Their confidence) – but all in vain!
For every time She shouted 'Fire!'
They only answered 'Little _____!'
And therefore when her Aunt returned,
Matilda, and the House, were _____.   50

*Putney, Hackney Downs, and Bow – places in the extreme
south-west, north, and east of London

†*The Second Mrs Tanqueray* – a dramatic four-act play, first
performed in 1893. The piece, by the playwright Arthur
Wing Pinero, was about a corrupt woman and her innocent
stepdaughter. It was very popular in its day.

 When you have finished, listen to the tape again and check your answers.

Comprehension check

1 Answer the following questions.

a. What kind of girl is Matilda?
b. Why does she call the fire brigade at the start of the poem?
c. What do the firemen do to the windows on the ballroom floor and the paintings in the house?
d. How does Matilda's aunt get them to go away?
e. Why doesn't Matilda go with her aunt to the theatre?
f. What do people do when Matilda asks for help at the end of the poem? Why?

2 Discuss these questions in groups. Use a dictionary if necessary.

a. Hilaire Belloc called 'Matilda' a Cautionary Verse. Why?
b. Do you think it was intended for children or adults to read?
c. Is the poem serious or funny? Do you think this makes the moral – or message – of the poem more or less effective?
d. Imagine you are a child. What message would you get from the poem? Write the moral of the story in ten words.
e. Underline the forced rhymes in the poem. What is the effect of these forced rhymes?
f. What do you notice about the author's use of capital letters? What is the effect of this?

What do you think?

– Nowadays in Britain, children are brought up with fewer rules than before. Is this the same in your country?
– What old rules for children's behaviour, dress, or table manners can you think of ?

Example
Don't put your elbows on the table.
Children should be seen and not heard.

– What do you think of these old rules? Should they be forgotten, or are they still useful today?

If you have enjoyed 'Matilda' and you would like to read about a little boy who swallowed pieces of string, or another boy who kept running away from his nurse and was eventually eaten by a lion, then we suggest you read more of Hilaire Belloc's *Cautionary Tales*.

5 Punishment and control

CARYL CHURCHILL *was born in London in 1938. She was educated at Oxford, where she became deeply involved in both politics and drama. She has written for the stage, radio, and television, and is probably the most well-known woman dramatist at present writing in Britain. Her plays reflect her strong commitment to radical politics and feminism, and they all address contemporary British social issues. Softcops was written in 1978. It was first performed by the Royal Shakespeare Company in 1984.*

Vocabulary 1

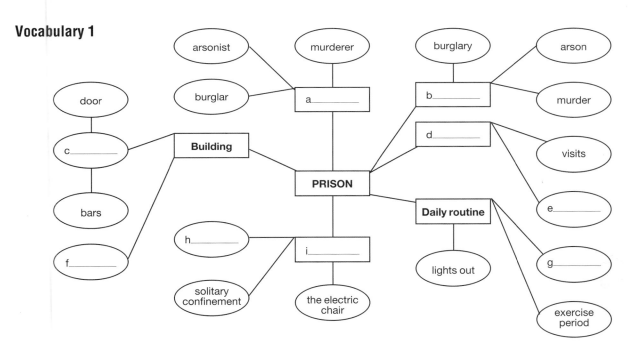

Use a dictionary to help you put each word from the box below into the correct space in the word spider above.

beating	**Crime**	uniform
cell	**Criminal**	**Punishment**
courtyard	**Rules**	roll call

Reading

'Cops' is slang for 'policemen', and Caryl Churchill's play *Softcops* – set in 19th-century France – is about different methods of treating criminals.

In earlier centuries, criminals were given harsh punishments in public as an example to others, but in the 19th century 'soft' methods of control – schools, hospitals, mental asylums, and orphanages – were introduced. *Softcops* looks at the difference between harsh physical punishment and 'soft' mental control.

You are going to read a scene from the play. In this scene, Pierre, a punishment expert, is showing a government minister round his new reform school for young criminals. At the start of the scene, boys in uniform enter silently and stand in a line. A new boy arrives, and Pierre describes the school to him.

1   Work on your own. Read the extract, and underline the sections which describe the school as follows:

Underline like this _____ any details about the school which you think are good.
Underline like this _ _ _ _ _ _ any details about the school which you think are bad.
Underline like this 〰〰〰 any details about the school which you think are not good or bad but interesting.

PIERRE Here you will live in a group called a family. The other boys are your brothers. Each family has a head, whom you will obey, and is divided into two sections, each with a second in command. You will have a number. You will answer to it at roll call three times a day. Your number is 321. This is your elder brother. He will stay with you all the time. And I will pay   5
constant attention to your case.

MINISTER Not one of you will be torn apart by horses. And I hope you're grateful. (*To* PIERRE) You may be on to something this time, my boy. Congratulations.

The MINISTER *and* PIERRE *go off.*   10

BOY Do they beat you?

BROTHER Not any more. If you do wrong they put you in a cell by yourself. And on the wall there's big black letters, God Sees You.

BOY That's all right. I don't believe in God.

BROTHER You will though.   15

BOY Don't mind what they do if they don't beat me.

BROTHER We preferred the beatings. But the cell is better for us.

BOY What sort of thing gets you into trouble?

BROTHER Speaking when you shouldn't. Walking out of step. Looking up when you should look down. *20*

BOY But what about stealing? And swearing? And hitting someone in the stomach? And setting fire?

BROTHER There's no time.

BOY I do what I like.

BROTHER But we like to do what we ought. *25*

BOY I don't.

The line walks round once in single file. The BOY *at the back steps backward leaving a space. The* BROTHER *puts the* BOY *in the space.*

BROTHER This is your place. We're going to the courtyard now and the monitor inspects our clothes. Then we go to where we sleep. At the first *30* drumroll you get undressed and stand by your hammock. At the second drumroll all the boys on the left on a count of one two three get into their hammocks and lie down. It's quite easy. Then the boys on the right do it. Then we go to sleep. You go to sleep lying on your back with your hands outside the cover. You always go to sleep straight away because you've *35* been working hard all day and then there's military exercise and gymnastics. We'll teach you. You can't talk now.

The BROTHER *takes his place at the head of the line.*

BOY What if you stay awake?

BROTHER You don't. *40*

BOY What if you do?

BROTHER If you stay awake, don't open your eyes.

The line starts to walk off. The BOY *steps out of his place and watches them. They stop, still leaving his space. They turn and look at him. Suddenly he runs and gets into place, gets into step as they go out.* *45*

---

2 Work in pairs. Compare notes with your partner. Decide which things in Pierre's reform school are good, and which are bad. Compare your views with those of other students.

Comprehension check

1 Read the scene from the play again and mark the following sentences T(true), F(false), or ?(don't know), according to the information in the text.

a. Each 'family' of boys has a leader and two deputy leaders.
b. There is roll call at breakfast, lunch, and dinner every day.
c. The boys never used to be beaten.
d. The new boy doesn't think God exists.
e. The boys prefer being put in a cell alone to being beaten.

f. Speaking during mealtimes is against the school rules.
g. The school rules are reasonable ones.
h. The boys are kept too busy to do really bad things.
i. The boys don't like to follow the school rules.
j. The boys must go to bed in their underwear.
k. The boys mustn't sleep with their hands under the bedcovers.
l. Boys can stay awake at night, as long as they keep their eyes closed.

2 Compare your answers with those of other students.

Vocabulary 2 and listening

1 Use a dictionary to check the meaning of the words in the box below.

docile	aggressive	rebellious
mesmerized	brainwashed	conformist
cowed	credulous	inquisitive

2 How would you describe the attitude of the prisoners to the school? Listen to the extract from the play and put the adjectives from the box above into the most appropriate column below.

T.5

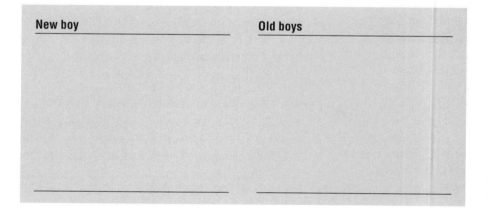

New boy	Old boys

What do you think?

Do you agree or disagree with the following statements? Read them and make notes, then discuss your opinions with other students.

1 'Soft' forms of control are not as good as harsh punishments.

2 Prisons shouldn't punish people for past crimes, but make them change their behaviour in the future.

3 Youngsters learn so much about crime in reform schools that most of them will end up later as adults in prison.

4 Crime is the product of an unjust society, and not the fault of the criminal.

5 Harsh punishments don't stop people committing crimes, they make criminals take care not to get caught.

6 Policemen have criminal minds, and they often think that they themselves are outside the law.

7 The police spend a lot of their time investigating less important crimes, and many top criminals never get caught or punished.

8 Prisons don't work and should be abolished.

9 A lot of people criticize the police, but they are doing a very necessary job in society.

10 Governments stop anti-establishment acts from being seen as political acts by calling them crimes. (All 'terrorists', for example, are really 'freedom fighters'.)

Writing

In Britain many people are worried by an apparent dramatic increase in crime over the past ten years or so.

Look at the table below. It gives the numbers of certain criminal offences recorded by the police in England and Wales in 1979 and 1989.
– Are all the crime figures going up at the same rate?

*including murder and manslaughter

	Homicide*	Burglary	Arson	Robbery
1979	629	544,037	11,640	12,482
1989	641	825,930	23,715	33,163

– What are the crime statistics like in your country?
– What do you think is the answer to the problem of crime?

Write 100 words explaining your views. (Use your pre-discussion notes to help you.)

6 Choosing a career

KAZUO ISHIGURO *was born in Japan in 1954, and came to Britain in 1960. He was educated at the universities of Kent and East Anglia. In 1980, he began publishing short stories and articles in magazines. Since then, he has written several novels and TV play scripts.* An Artist of the Floating World, *published in 1986, won the Whitbread Book of the Year award. A later novel,* The Remains of the Day, *won the Booker Prize in 1989. Kazuo Ishiguro is generally regarded as one of the most talented writers in Britain today.*

Discussion

1   Work in pairs. First find out if your partner is still a student, or already has a job. Then interview your partner using the following questions.

    a. What job did you want to do when you were a young child?

    b. What job do you intend to go into when you leave school/university/college?
       or
       What job did you go into when you left school/university/college?

    c. What job do/did your parents want you to do? Are/Were they happy with your choice of career?

2   Report your interviews to other student pairs.

Vocabulary

1   The words in the box all occur in the texts you are going to read. Use a dictionary to check what they mean.

deliberation (*n*)	depraved (*adj*)	eavesdrop (*v*)
kindle (*v*)	lap (*n*)	nod (*v*)
perplexed (*adj*)	pitfall (*n*)	resolve (*n*)
squalor (*n*)	whim (*n*)	

2 Read the following sentences. Replace each underlined word with one of the nouns, verbs, or adjectives from the box. (Don't forget to put the nouns and verbs into the correct form.)

a. We <u>verbed</u> on the conversation from outside the door.

b. The cat sat on my <u>noun</u> all evening.

c. I asked if he wanted a coffee, and he <u>verbed</u> .

d. She lives in one small room, with her six children, in total <u>noun</u> .

e. I was <u>adjective</u> when I couldn't find my key. I was sure it was in my pocket.

f. The boy <u>verbed</u> a fire by rubbing two sticks together.

g. He soon forgot all about painting his room purple. It was only a passing <u>noun</u> .

h. He takes drugs, drinks a lot, and has a different girlfriend every night. He really is <u>adjective</u> .

i. They have invaded our country and killed our people, but our <u>noun</u> to win the war is stronger than before.

j. I don't think this plan will work. It has too many <u>nouns</u> .

k. It was not easy to decide on the winner, but, after some <u>noun</u> we agreed on Kevin Costner's *Dances with Wolves*.

Reading 1

Kazuo Ishiguro's book *An Artist of the Floating World* is about Masuji, an old Japanese artist. In the extract you are going to read, Masuji remembers the time when, as a young man, he was asked to go to the formal reception room of the family house, to discuss his future career plans with his mother and father.

1 Before you read Extract 1, work in pairs and try to guess the answers to these questions.

a. What will Masuji say to his businessman father about wanting to be a professional artist?

b. How will Masuji's father feel about his son's plans? What will he say?

c. What will Sachiko (Masuji's mother) do? What will she say?

2 Now read Extract 1 and check your predictions.

Extract 1

THEN, with some deliberation, my father picked up three or four of my paintings and held them in both hands as though to test their weight. He turned his gaze towards me and said: 'Masuji, your mother here was under the impression that you wished to pursue painting as a profession. Has there perhaps been some misunderstanding on her part?' 5

I lowered my eyes and remained silent. Then I heard my mother's voice beside me, almost whispering, say: 'He's still very young. I'm sure it's just a childish whim of his.'

There was a pause, then my father said: 'Tell me, Masuji, have you any idea what kind of a world artists inhabit?' 10

I remained silent, looking at the floor before me.

'Artists', my father's voice continued, 'live in squalor and poverty. They inhabit a world which gives them every temptation to become weak-willed and depraved. Am I not right, Sachiko?'

'Naturally. Yet perhaps there are one or two who are able to pursue an 15 artistic career and yet avoid such pitfalls.'

'Of course, there are exceptions,' my father said. My eyes were still lowered, but I could tell from his voice that he was again nodding in his perplexed manner. 'The handful with extraordinary resolve and character. But I'm afraid our son here is far from being such a person. Indeed, quite the 20 contrary. It is our duty to protect him from such dangers. We do, after all, wish him to become someone we can be proud of, don't we?'

'Of course,' my mother said.

I looked up quickly. The candle had burned half-way down its length and the flame was sharply illuminating one side of my father's face. He had now 25 placed the paintings on his lap, and I noticed how his fingers were moving impatiently along their edges.

'Masuji,' he said, 'you may leave us now. I wish to speak with your mother.'

Reading 2

1 Before you read Extract 2, work in pairs and try to guess the answers to these questions.

a. What will Masuji's father do to stop him from becoming an artist?
b. What will Masuji's mother do? What will she say?
c. Will Masuji change his plans because of what his parents do?

2 Now read Extract 2 and check your predictions.

Extract 2

I CAN REMEMBER a little later that night, coming across my mother in the darkness. In all likelihood, it was in one of the corridors that I encountered her, though I do not remember this. Neither do I remember why I was wandering around the house in the dark, but it was certainly not in order to eavesdrop on my parents – for I do recall being resolved to pay no heed to 5 what occurred in the reception room after my departure. In those days, of course, houses were all badly lit, so it was not at all unusual that we should stand in the dark and converse. I could make out my mother's figure in front of me, but could not see her face.

'There's a smell of burning around the house,' I remarked. 10

'Burning?' My mother was silent for a while, then she said: 'No. I don't think so. It must be your imagination, Masuji.'

'I smelt burning,' I said. 'There, I just caught it again. Is Father still in the reception room?'

'Yes. He's working on something.' 15

'Whatever he's doing in there,' I said, 'it doesn't bother me in the least.'

My mother made no sound, so I added: 'The only thing Father's succeeded in kindling is my ambition.'

Listening and discussion

T.6

Look at the illustration on page 36 as you listen to Extract 1. Then listen to Extract 2. If you were designing an illustration for this passage, what would you include in it?

Writing

1 Work in groups of three pairs. Each pair should take a section of the texts above and rewrite it as a film script. Divide up the texts as follows.

Extract 1 lines 1–14 Pair A   **Extract 2** lines 1–18 Pair C
              lines 15–29 Pair B

Try to keep the Japanese flavour and to express some of the characters' unspoken thoughts. Look at the example on page 38.

Example

INT.* RECEPTION ROOM - NIGHT

The paper-walled room is in half darkness. MASUJI is kneeling in front of his FATHER. MASUJI's FATHER is sitting cross-legged next to a large candle. Many paintings are lying spread out on the floor in front of him. MASUJI's MOTHER is a little further away, in the shadows. MASUJI's FATHER picks up one of the paintings and looks at it carefully.

                    FATHER
              (clearing his throat)
Masuji. Your mother here was under the impression that you wished to pursue painting as a profession.
              (long pause)
Has there perhaps been some misunderstanding on her part?

---

*INT. Interior (an indoor
scene)
 EXT. Exterior (an outdoor
scene)

If you like, you could set the same basic story in a different country – your own perhaps, or one that you know well. How does this change the atmosphere and the way the characters behave and communicate?

2 Compare your finished section of script with those prepared by other pairs. Are there any changes you need to make so that the script fits together as a whole?

3 Try acting out your finished script. If you have a video camera, you could film it.

> *An Artist of the Floating World* is quite a short book. If you are interested in the rest of the artist's story, we suggest you read the whole novel.

7 The tale of a river

STEVIE SMITH *was born in Hull in 1902. She was christened Florence Margaret Smith, but later changed her name. When she was three, she moved to London with her mother and sister to live at her aunt's house, where she stayed for the rest of her life. After leaving school she worked as a secretary in a publisher's office until 1953, when she retired to look after her aunt who was by then an invalid. 'The River God' comes from the* Collected Poems *(1975). Stevie Smith died in 1971.*

Vocabulary

1 Add the extra letters to each word on the left (at the beginning, in the middle, or at the end) to make a new word which matches the definition in brackets on the right. Use a dictionary if you want.

a. sell + y + m = _____*smelly*_____ (having an unpleasant smell)

b. red + e = _____ (a plant that grows at the edge of a river or lake)

c. less + b = _____ (to give God's protection to)

d. bat + e + h = _____ (a poetic word for swim)

e. we + r + i = _____ (a low dam, built across a river, to control the movement of the water)

f. own + r + d = _____ (to die through being unable to breathe underwater)

g. old + b = _____ (adventurous)

h. we + d + e = _____ (an underwater plant)

i. fat + o + l = _____ (to move slowly and without effort through water)

j. far + e = _____ (what someone who is afraid feels)

k. owning + l + c = _____ (doing silly things for fun)

l. low + f = _____ (The Tiber, the Thames, and the Seine all do this through capital cities.)

2 Use the definitions on the right to help you sort out the anagrams on the left.

a. bespelb = ___*pebbles*___ (small, round stones)

b. uflo = _____ (really unpleasant)

c. lirymre = _____ (a poetic word for happily)

d. torycran ot = _____ (two words meaning in opposition to)

e. lynpet fo og = _____ (a slang expression meaning lots of energy)

f. fficl = _____ (a high piece of land which overlooks the sea)

g. deb = _____ (the bottom of a river or of the sea)

Listening

1 Below is a gapped version of a poem by Stevie Smith. Listen and fill in the gaps.

The River God
(of the River Mimram in Hertfordshire)

T.7

I may be smelly and I may be _____,
Rough in my pebbles, reedy in my pools,
But where my fish _____ by I bless their swimming
And I like the people to bathe in me, especially women.
But I can drown the fools   5
Who bathe too _____ to the weir, contrary to rules.
And they take a long time drowning
As I _____ them up now and then in a spirit of clowning.
Hi yih, yippity-yap, merrily I _____,
_____ I may be an _____ foul river but I have plenty of _____.   10
Once there was a lady who was too _____
She bathed in me by the tall black cliff where the water runs _____,
So I brought her down here
To be my beautiful dear.
_____ will she stay with me will she stay   15
This beautiful lady, or will she _____ away?
She lies in my beautiful deep river bed with many a weed
To _____ her, and many a waving reed.
_____ who would guess what a beautiful white face lies there
Waiting for me to smooth and wash away the fear   20
She looks at me with. Hi yih, do not let her
_____. There is _____ one on earth who does not forget her
Now. They say I am a foolish _____ smelly river
But they do not _____ of my wide original bed
Where the lady waits, with her _____ sleepy head.   25
If she wishes to _____ I will not forgive her.

2 Discuss the following questions in pairs.

a. What vowel sound do all the words in the gaps contain?
b. What do these repeated vowel sounds make you think of?

Comprehension check

1 Read the following summary of the poem and fill in the gaps with appropriate words. (Note: You don't *always* have to use words from the poem. Sometimes, in fact, you'll *have* to find your own words!)

The poem is told from the (a) _____'s point of view. It describes how he likes people – particularly (b) _____ – swimming in the river. It explains how, for fun, he (c) _____ people who swim too near the (d) _____. In particular it tells the story of how he caught one woman who (e) _____ near the weir and took her down to the (f) _____ to be his (g) _____. She is (h) _____ of him, but he does not want her to (i) _____ him. At the end of the poem the River God complains that people think he is (j) _____, (k) _____, and (l) _____, but that few people realize he has a beautiful woman (m) _____ for him on the river bed.

2 Discuss the following questions in pairs.

a. 'Rough and ready' is an idiomatic expression which means 'simple, because it's been done in a hurry' (e.g. 'Lunch is a bit rough and ready today, I'm afraid.'). Can you find a line in the poem which plays with this expression?

b. 'Yapping' is the noise made by a small dog. It also means talking noisily and foolishly. Bearing this in mind, what impression do the nonsense words 'Hi yih, yippity-yap' (line 9) and 'Hi yih' (line 21) give you about the River God?

c. '... the tall black cliff where the water runs cold' (line 12) refers back to something which has been mentioned earlier in the poem. What is it?

d. What different meanings does the word 'bed' have in line 17?

e. Has the woman been under the river for a long or a short time according to lines 22–23?

f. Which adjectives describe the River God, and which describe the lady?

g. Why do you think the River God loves the woman?

h. What do you think is meant by the phrase 'wide original bed' in line 24? Why is the river no longer wide now? How does the River God feel about this?

Points of style

1 Find the lines where the following words are repeated.

   a. old (line 1)   c. beautiful (line 14)
   b. smelly (line 1)   d. lady (line 11)

2 There are also many near repetitions in the poem (i.e. different forms of the same word). Can you find the near repetitions of the following words?

   a. bathe (lines 4 and 6)   d. fools (line 5)
   b. reedy (line 2)   e. waiting (line 20)
   c. drown (line 5)

3 How many repeated phrases can you find in the poem (e.g. *I may be* smelly and *I may be* old)? How do the repetitions and near repetitions suggest the sound and strength of a river?

4 Look at the rhymes in the poem.

   a. Which lines rhyme with line 1?   c. Which lines rhyme with line 20?
   b. Which lines rhyme with line 2?

   How does the pattern of the rhymes in the whole poem suggest the patterns made by water in a river as it flows onwards?

Writing

Think of a geographical feature (a mountain, river, lake, or sea). It can be world famous or just well known in your country. You could choose something that you personally know about which isn't very well known.

Write a poem or a short prose passage from the point of view of the 'spirit' of your chosen feature.

   – How do you feel about men and women?
   – What do people think of you?
   – What do you remember?

> Many of Stevie Smith's poems are humorous and written in colloquial English. Many are also illustrated with her own comic drawings. We strongly recommend you read more of her poetry if you have enjoyed 'The River God'.

8 New buildings and old

ANNE TURNER *is a contemporary Scottish short story writer. Her work has been published in many periodicals and has also been anthologized and broadcast. 'Building for the Future' was first published in 1977 in the Scottish Arts Council* Anthology *Scottish Short Stories.*

What do you think?

Discuss the following questions in groups.

– What is your favourite building? Why do you like it?
– Are there any buildings you hate? Why?
– Would you prefer to live in a modern or an old building? Why?

Vocabulary 1

Match a word in **A** with a definition in **B**.

A	B
1 the spire	a. to be completely destroyed
2 absent	b. the pointed top on a church tower
3 amazed	c. the people who usually go to a church
4 commercialism	d. very surprised
5 the congregation	e. not there
6 to be demolished	f. money-making
7 dismayed	g. to be in danger, at risk
8 irreplaceable	h. shocked and discouraged
9 a steeple	i. which cannot be replaced
10 to be at stake	j. unimportant things
11 trivialities	k. a tall tower with a spire on top

Reading 1

The dialogue below is taken (without surrounding narration and description) from a short story called 'Building for the Future'.

1 Read the dialogue and answer these questions:

a. Who do you think is speaking?
b. Where do you think they are?
c. What do you think the story is about?

'I'm amazed. Amazed and dismayed – '

'Name and address. Please address the Chair.'

'I'm dismayed at half the night being wasted on trivialities when the future of our beautiful old church and its irreplaceable spire is at stake!'

'Absolutely irreplaceable.'

'Our spire has stood for centuries as a symbol and an inspiration. The Reverend Whittaker is absent with bronchitis tonight, but we members of his congregation will not stand by and let our steeple be demolished. We will never allow its place to be taken by ugly commercialism!'

---

2 Now read the dialogue again, this time with some surrounding narration and description. Are the guesses you made in **1** correct? Are there any surprises?

A serious, fat, middle-aged woman stood up and raised her hand.

'I'm amazed,' she said, looking round the hall. 'Amazed and dismayed – '

'Name and address,' said the Chairman. 'Please address the Chair.'

She gave her name and address as she was asked. 'I'm dismayed at half the night being wasted on trivialities when the future of our beautiful old church and its irreplaceable spire is at stake!'

'Absolutely irreplaceable,' said one of the men.

'Our spire has stood for centuries as a symbol and an inspiration,' she continued. 'The Reverend Whittaker is absent with bronchitis tonight, but we members of his congregation will not stand by and let our steeple be demolished. We will never allow its place to be taken by ugly commercialism!' She pointed at all the plans fixed to the wall.

There were a few cheers and some stamping at the end of this speech.

Vocabulary 2

Choose the best explanation for the underlined words below.

1 Queen Victoria, who rarely smiled in public, always looked very <u>stern</u>.

   a. serious ✓   b. beautiful   c. rich   d. ugly

2 She <u>rose</u> slowly from the sofa and left the room.

   a. fell   b. stood up   c. jumped   d. walked

3 She <u>glared</u> at her young brother when he called her 'fatty'.

   a. looked sadly   b. looked lovingly   c. looked angrily
   d. looked happily

4 He <u>deprecated</u> his daughter's idea of working for a year in Mongolia because it was so far away.

   a. criticized   b. loved   c. hated   d. destroyed

5 There was a wide <u>array</u> of cakes in the shop window.

   a. box   b. plate   c. selection   d. shelf

6 Italians often use a lot of <u>gestures</u> when they speak.

   a. bad words   b. long words   c. facial movements
   d. hand and arm movements

7 He asked her to help him with the cooking and she said she'd be happy to <u>oblige</u>.

   a. say no   b. do what he wanted   c. make him do it
   d. tell someone else to do it

8 Winston Churchill broadcast many <u>stirring</u> speeches on the radio during World War II.

   a. boring   b. funny   c. sad   d. inspiring

9 There was a poster of Sylvester Stallone <u>tacked</u> to the wall by her bed.

   a. glued   b. stuck   c. pinned   d. sellotaped

10 They <u>rounded off</u> the meal with coffee and brandy.

   a. finished   b. started   c. continued   d. interrupted

Reading 2

1 Below is the original text, exactly as it appears in the short story 'Building for the Future' by Anne Turner. What differences do you notice between this version and the one given in Reading 1? Which version do you prefer?

A STERN MATRONLY person rose to speak, commanding attention with a gesture.

'I'm amazed,' she announced, glaring round the hall. 'Amazed and dismayed –'

'Name and address,' sighed the Chairman. 'Please address the Chair.' 5

She obliged haughtily. 'I'm dismayed at half the night being wasted on trivialities when the future of our beautiful old church and its irreplaceable spire is at stake!'

'Absolutely irreplaceable,' agreed a gentlemanly voice.

'Our spire has stood for centuries as a symbol and an inspiration,' she 10 went on forcefully. 'The Reverend Whittaker is absent with bronchitis tonight, but we members of his congregation will not stand by and let our steeple be demolished. We will never allow its place to be taken by ugly commercialism!' Her arm swept out and deprecated the array of plans tacked to the wall. 15

Localized cheers and stamping rounded off this stirring speech.

2 Look at the passage again and answer the questions.

a. Find six words in the text ending in -ly. Decide if they are adjectives or adverbs. What do they mean? How are they pronounced?

b. Which verbs are used in the text in place of the verb 'said'? Why are they used instead of 'said'?

Listening

T.8

Listen to the passage as you read it again.

Discussion

Think about your own country/city/town, and discuss the following questions.

– Have there been any new building developments there recently? How do local people feel about them?

– Were any historic buildings demolished in the past which people now feel should have been preserved?

– Are there any historic buildings in danger at present? What is being done to preserve them?

9 Effects of war

DENISE LEVERTOV *is an American citizen, although she was born in Britain in 1923. She grew up in Britain and was educated at home. Her first volume of poems, published in 1946, was based on her experiences working in The British Hospital in Paris during the Second World War. She married an American writer and emigrated to America in 1948. In 1955 she became a US citizen. 'What Were They Like?' comes from the anthology* To Stay Alive, *first published in 1966.*

Vocabulary

Use your dictionary to help you choose the word which best fits the gap in each of the following sentences. (Be careful! The three words in each group are very close in meaning.)

1 Around the garden, hanging from various trees, beautiful Chinese paper _____ shone in the night.

    a. lanterns ✓   b. torches   c. spotlights

2 It was spring, and the _____ on all the trees were beginning to open.

    a. shoots   b. sprouts   c. buds

3 I don't think they should shoot elephants for their _____.

    a. bone   b. ivory   c. horn

4 Max's copy of the Mona Lisa was so good it was very difficult to _____ it from the real thing.

    a. differ   b. contrast   c. distinguish

5 He felt very _____ when he lost his job because of the economic recession.

    a. tart   b. bitter   c. acid

6 When the fire had died down there was nothing left of the garden shed but a few _____ sticks of wood.

    a. charred   b. singed   c. overdone

7 All the cherry trees in the street were covered in lovely pink _____.

    a. bloom   b. blossom   c. flora

8 Lots of Romanian _____ were there, hoping to sell their bowls, tablecloths, and dolls to rich western tourists.

    a. rustics   b. countrymen   c. peasants

9 I read until late, and lots of _____ gathered at my window, attracted by the light from my reading lamp.

    a. butterflies   b. dragonflies   c. moths

10 The olive trees were planted up the hillside in _____.

    a. terraces   b. stairs   c. balconies

11 The ancient Greek poet Homer is famous for the two _____ poems he wrote – *The Odyssey* and *The Iliad*.

    a. adventure   b. epic   c. saga

12 Rice is grown in China in _____.

    a. groves   b. paddy fields   c. plantations

What do you think?

You are going to read a poem by Denise Levertov about Vietnam. It was written in 1966. Before you read, mark a cross (×) on the different scales below where you think the main emphasis of the poem will be each time.

Example
If you think the poem will be pro-American, mark the first scale like this.

pro-American   ◄—**X**——————————►   pro-Vietnamese

pro-American	◄————————►	pro-Vietnamese
gentle	◄————————►	aggressive
sad	◄————————►	happy
forward-looking	◄————————►	nostalgic
ugly	◄————————►	beautiful
playful	◄————————►	serious

Compare your marked scales in pairs.

Reading and listening

1 Read the poem.

What Were They Like?

1) Did the people of Vietnam
   use lanterns of stone?
2) Did they hold ceremonies

*reverence – revere, celebrate

   to reverence* the opening of buds?
3) Were they inclined to quiet laughter?   5
4) Did they use bone and ivory,
   jade and silver, for ornament?
5) Had they an epic poem?
6) Did they distinguish between speech and singing?

1) Sir, their light hearts turned to stone.   10
   It is not remembered whether in gardens

*illumined – illuminated, lit

   stone lanterns illumined* pleasant ways.
2) Perhaps they gathered once to delight in blossom,
   but after the children were killed
   there were no more buds.   15
3) Sir, laughter is bitter to the burned mouth.
4) A dream ago, perhaps. Ornament is for joy.
   All the bones were charred.
5) It is not remembered. Remember,
   most were peasants; their life   20
   was in rice and bamboo.
   When peaceful clouds were reflected in the paddies
   and the water buffalo stepped surely along terraces,
   maybe fathers told their sons old tales.
   When bombs smashed those mirrors   25
   there was time only to scream.
6) There is an echo yet
   of their speech which was like a song.
   It was reported their singing resembled
   the flight of moths in moonlight.   30
   Who can say? It is silent now.

2 Were your predictions about main emphasis correct? What are your impressions of the poem now?

3 Listen to the poem being read twice. Which version do you prefer, A or B? Why?

Comprehension check

Look at lines 10–31 of the poem again, and answer the following questions.

1 What stopped the Vietnamese holding ceremonies to celebrate the coming of spring?
2 Why didn't the Vietnamese laugh?
3 What stopped the Vietnamese wearing jade, silver, bone, and ivory ornaments?
4 Where and when might Vietnamese fathers have told stories to their sons?
5 What put an end to any story-telling?
6 Was Vietnamese speech like singing?
7 Why is the singing and speaking 'silent now'?

Points of style

The following lines from the poem all contain richly figurative language. Look at the underlined words in each line and decide what they mean. (Sometimes more than one meaning is possible.)

1 (line 10) Sir, their light hearts turned to stone.
   a. their cheerful hearts became heavy with sadness
   b. their mad hearts became aggressive
   c. their happy hearts became unfeeling

2 (lines 14–15) . . . after the children were killed there were no more buds.
   a. unopened flowers on the trees
   b. young babies
   c. things to look forward to

3 (line 18) All the bones were charred.
   a. Burnt human bones were everywhere.
   b. All the bone and ivory ornaments were spoiled.
   c. People threw all their ornaments into the fire.

4 (lines 25–26) When bombs smashed those mirrors there was time only to scream.
   a. shattered women's hand mirrors
   b. dropped on the paddy fields
   c. broke the reflections of clouds in the water

5 (lines 27–28) There is an echo yet of their speech which was like a song.
   a. a fading memory
   b. a repetitive copy
   c. a weak reminder

What do you think?

Discuss these questions in pairs.

1 What are the questions trying to find out? Do the answers really help? Why do some answers begin with 'Sir' do you think?

2 Find examples of passive verb forms in the poem (e.g. 'Were they inclined. . . ?'). Why do you think the poet uses so many passive verbs?

3 The following phrases from the poem do not seem typically English. Why do you think they are so strange?

'Ornament is for joy.'
'Laughter is bitter to the burnt mouth.'
'Their singing resembled/the flight of moths in moonlight.'

4 In wartime the enemy is often 'dehumanized' by the media, being described as monsters or animals, for propaganda purposes. How does this poem present the enemy?

Writing

The US involvement in Vietnam ended in a cease-fire agreement in 1973. It was not, however, the end of the Vietnamese problem.

– After the cease-fire, many Vietnamese left Vietnam in small boats, hoping to make a new life in any country which would take them. Many died on the open sea. The lucky ones who survived and were taken in faced serious problems of cultural adaptation and integration. Many got no further than 'first asylum' refugee camps in places like Hong Kong.

– After the cease-fire, all US troops remaining in Vietnam were evacuated. Many American soldiers went back home physically or psychologically damaged by their experiences in the war. Many have found it very hard to readjust and to integrate back into civilian life in North America.

Imagine you are either one of the Vietnamese 'boat people', or one of the US army veterans from the war in Vietnam, or a refugee or army veteran from any other war. Write a poem or a piece of prose about the effects of war. (If you or a member of your family was once involved in a war, you might want to write about your or their experience.)

Story of a life

CHARLOTTE BRONTË *was born in Yorkshire in 1816 into a truly remarkable literary family. She and her two sisters, Emily and Anne, were all writers of great talent, although it is probably Charlotte who is remembered today as the most gifted. Their family was poor, and in their early years the sisters tried to earn money by working as governesses and later by opening a village school. Eventually they gave up teaching and turned to writing, first poetry and then novels. Because of the difficulties of writing as women in the nineteenth century, the sisters wrote under the pseudonyms of Currer, Ellis, and Acton Bell. Charlotte published three novels before her death in 1855.* Jane Eyre *was first published in 1847.*

Vocabulary

Use the words in brackets after each sentence to make a new word which fits the gap. Use a dictionary (and the given letters in the gapped words) to help you.

1 He's suffering from the d_e_l_u_s_i_o_n that she's in love with him, when actually she loves his brother. (delude)

2 He's much more m _ _ _ u _ _ r than his brother, although he seldom does any sport. (muscle)

3 The best way to find a good restaurant is through personal _ _ _ _ m _ _ _ _ _ t _ _ _ . (recommend)

4 The changes were already _ _ r _ _ p _ i _ _ _ before the war, but they became even more obvious afterwards. (perceive)

5 The soldiers fighting from behind the castle b _ _ _ _ _ m _ _ ts were well protected from the enemy. (battle)

6 Although I was born in England, I'm now a Canadian _ _ s _ _ _ _ t. (reside)

7 She lived with the family as a _ _ v _ _ n _ s _ and taught the children Maths and French. (govern)

8 He grew his hair long in _ e _ _ _ n _ e of his father, who had told him to have it cut. (defy)

9 This part of the hospital doesn't receive any money from the government. It is financed by ____ it _ b __ donations. (charity)

10 It's a very old e__a_____e__. They've been making and selling biscuits and cakes there since 1891. (establish)

11 In late summer there was an ___n__n__ of fruit and vegetables, so they had to hire extra people to pick them all. (abundant)

Looking at plot

The chart on page 54 shows the main plot of *Jane Eyre* by Charlotte Brontë. The large boxes show the five different places that Jane lives in and people she lives with. These provide the background for the development of the plot. The smaller boxes show the important events or emotions which lead Jane (_____) and Mr Rochester (____) from one setting to another.

Use the chart to help you fill in the gaps in the sentences below with an appropriate word or phrase.

1 Jane Eyre has a largely _____ childhood.

2 She is treated _____ by her aunt and cousins.

3 Her aunt spends _____ money on sending her away to school.

4 Jane is a _____ student.

5 Jane is _____ with her work at Lowood Academy.

6 Mr Rochester _____ Jane to _____ a French girl.

7 When Mr Rochester proposes to Jane, she _____ that he is already married.

8 When Jane runs away from Thornfield Hall, she _____ Mr Rochester where she is going.

9 When the Rivers rescue her, Jane _____ that they are her cousins.

10 When Jane returns to Mr Rochester, she has _____ money.

11 When Jane returns to Mr Rochester, his mad wife is _____.

12 When Jane returns to Mr Rochester, he is _____.

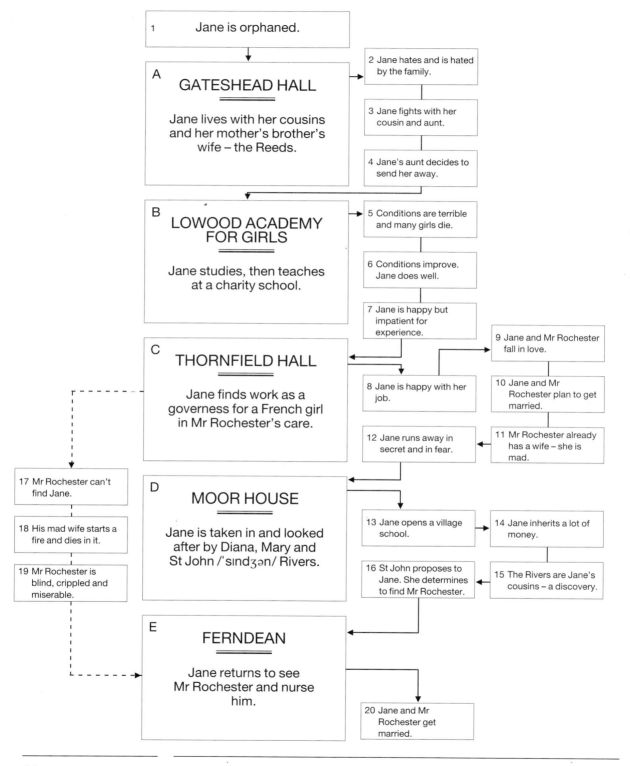

1 Jane is orphaned.

A GATESHEAD HALL

Jane lives with her cousins and her mother's brother's wife – the Reeds.

2 Jane hates and is hated by the family.

3 Jane fights with her cousin and aunt.

4 Jane's aunt decides to send her away.

B LOWOOD ACADEMY FOR GIRLS

Jane studies, then teaches at a charity school.

5 Conditions are terrible and many girls die.

6 Conditions improve. Jane does well.

7 Jane is happy but impatient for experience.

C THORNFIELD HALL

Jane finds work as a governess for a French girl in Mr Rochester's care.

8 Jane is happy with her job.

9 Jane and Mr Rochester fall in love.

10 Jane and Mr Rochester plan to get married.

11 Mr Rochester already has a wife – she is mad.

12 Jane runs away in secret and in fear.

D MOOR HOUSE

Jane is taken in and looked after by Diana, Mary and St John /ˈsɪndʒən/ Rivers.

13 Jane opens a village school.

14 Jane inherits a lot of money.

15 The Rivers are Jane's cousins – a discovery.

16 St John proposes to Jane. She determines to find Mr Rochester.

17 Mr Rochester can't find Jane.

18 His mad wife starts a fire and dies in it.

19 Mr Rochester is blind, crippled and miserable.

E FERNDEAN

Jane returns to see Mr Rochester and nurse him.

20 Jane and Mr Rochester get married.

Reading

These extracts from *Jane Eyre* are not in the order they appear in the book. Read the extracts and decide where they come in the book. Look back at the chart and match each extract below with the most appropriate box (large or small). Give reasons for your decision.

Extract 1

'GREAT GOD! – what delusion has come over me? What sweet mad-ness has seized me?'

'No delusion – no madness: your mind, sir, is too strong for delusion, your health too sound for frenzy.'

'And where is the speaker? Is it only a voice? Oh! I *cannot* see, but I must   5
feel, or my heart will stop and my brain burst. Whatever, whoever you are, be perceptible to the touch, or I cannot live!'

He groped; I arrested his wandering hand, and prisoned it in both mine.

'Her very fingers!' he cried; 'her small, slight fingers! If so, there must be more of her.'   10

The muscular hand broke from my custody; my arm was seized, my shoulder, neck, waist – I was entwined and gathered to him.

'Is it Jane? *What* is it? This is her shape – this is her size –'

'And this her voice,' I added. 'She is all here: her heart, too. God bless you, sir! I am glad to be so near you again.'   15

'Jane Eyre! – Jane Eyre!' was all he said.

Extract 2

THE MANIAC BELLOWED: she parted her shaggy locks from her vis-age, and gazed wildly at her visitors. I recognized well that purple face – those bloated features. Mrs Poole advanced.

'Keep out of the way,' said Mr Rochester, thrusting her aside: 'she has no   20
knife now, I suppose? and I'm on my guard.'

'One never knows what she has, sir: she is so cunning: it is not in mortal discretion to fathom her craft.'

'We had better leave her,' whispered Mason.

'Go to the devil!' was his brother-in-law's recommendation.   25

''Ware!' cried Grace. The three gentlemen retreated simultaneously. Mr Rochester flung me behind him: the lunatic sprang and grappled his throat viciously, and laid her teeth to his cheek: they struggled.

Extract 3

YOU LIVE just below – do you mean at that house with the battle-ments?' pointing to Thornfield Hall, on which the moon cast a hoary   30
gleam, bringing it out distinct and pale from the woods, that, by contrast with the western sky, now seemed one mass of shadow.

'Yes, sir.'

'Whose house is it?'

'Mr Rochester's.'   *35*
'Do you know Mr Rochester?'
'No, I have never seen him.'
'He is not resident, then?'
'No.'
'Can you tell me where he is?'   *40*
'I cannot.'
'You are not a servant at the Hall, of course. You are – ' He stopped, ran
his eye over my dress, which as usual, was quite simple – a black merino
cloak, a black beaver bonnet; neither of them half fine enough for a lady's-
maid. He seemed puzzled to decide what I was – I helped him.   *45*
'I am the governess.'
'Ah, the governess!' he repeated; 'deuce* take me if I had not forgotten!
The governess!'

*deuce – the devil, used as an
exclamation

Extract 4

'MISS TEMPLE, Miss Temple, what – *what* is that girl with curled hair?
Red hair, ma'am, curled all over?' And extending his cane he pointed   *50*
to the awful object, his hand shaking as he did so.
'It is Julia Severn,' replied Miss Temple very quietly.
'Julia Severn, ma'am! And why has she, or any other, curled hair? Why, in
defiance of every precept and principle of this house, does she conform to
the world so openly – here in an evangelical, charitable establishment – as *55*
to wear her hair one mass of curls?'
'Julia's hair curls naturally,' returned Miss Temple still more quietly.
'Naturally! Yes, but we are not to conform to nature. I wish these girls to
be the children of Grace: and why that abundance? I have again and again
intimated that I desire the hair to be arranged closely, modestly, plainly.   *60*
Miss Temple, that girl's hair must be cut off entirely; I will send a barber tomorrow: and I see others who have far too much of the excrescence* – that
tall girl, tell her to turn round. Tell all the first form to rise up and direct their
faces to the wall.'

*excrescence – an
unnecessary extra part of
something

🔑━0

Comprehension check

T.10

Listen to the extracts. As you listen, look at the sentences below. Decide if
they are true (T) or false (F). Discuss your answers with a partner. You may
want to look back at the extracts to check some details.

Extract 1

1 Mr Rochester is blind.
2 Mr Rochester is mad.
3 Mr Rochester is terribly happy to see Jane.
4 Jane has just returned from somewhere unexpectedly.

Extract 2

5 The madwoman isn't dangerous.
6 Grace Poole is the madwoman's nurse.
7 Jane has seen the madwoman before.
8 Mr Rochester attacks the madwoman.

Extract 3

9 Jane and Mr Rochester are standing on a hill.
10 It is early in the morning.
11 Mr Rochester doesn't live at Thornfield Hall.
12 Mr Rochester has forgotten about the existence of the governess.

Extract 4

13 The man is a school teacher.
14 Miss Temple doesn't agree with the man.
15 Many of the girls have long hair.
16 Miss Temple is kind to the girls.

Points of style

In the extracts there are a number of words and expressions which are not found in modern colloquial English. They are either literary or archaic words or phrases which give Charlotte Brontë's prose its own individual style.

Read the sentences and phrases below and match them with sentences or phrases from the extracts which have the same meaning. (The sentences are in the same order as in the extracts.)

Extract 1

1 Am I going mad?

_____

2 . . . you are too healthy to go mad.

_____

3 He felt around blindly with his hand, which I picked up and held in both of mine.

_____

4 He pulled his strong hand away from mine. . .

_____

5 He put his arms around me and pulled me towards him.

_____

Extract 2

6 The madwoman gave a loud, deep shout. . .

_____

7 She pushed her long, untidy hair out of her face. . .

_____

8 . . . pushing her to one side. . .

_____

9 It's impossible for a normal person to understand her tricks.

_____

10 . . . the madwoman jumped and attacked his neck. . .

_____

Extract 3

11 . . .which was lit up by the greyish-white light of the moon. . .

_____

12 He seemed unsure about me. . .

_____

Extract 4

13 I've told you many times. . .

_____

Writing

You work for a publishing company that produces modernized versions of the classics of English literature for intermediate students of English. Look at Extract 1 again. Using the sentences and phrases from the previous exercise to help you, rewrite it for the modernized version of _Jane Eyre_.

> In this unit you have explored the main plot of the novel _Jane Eyre_. If you are interested in discovering more about the relationship between the various characters, there is a 1943 film of _Jane Eyre_ which you may find interesting to watch.

11 A voice from the past

The novelist and short story writer, RK (RASIPURAM KRISHNASWAMI) NARAYAN, *was born in Madras, in Southern India, in 1907. His first novel,* Swami and Friends, *was published in 1935. In this novel, he created the imaginary small town of Malgudi, which appears in several later novels and short stories. Narayan is the most famous contemporary Indian writer working in English, and he has won many literary prizes in India, Britain, and the United States. 'Old Man of the Temple' comes from* Under the Banyan Tree, *a collection of his short stories first published in 1985.*

Vocabulary

Use a dictionary to replace the underlined words in each of the following sentences with a noun, adjective, verb, or adverb from the box on page 60.

1 From the other side of the room I could see one of the pictures was hanging out of its proper position (*a*), not exactly vertical like the others.

2 He shook my hand with lots of energy (___) and said how happy he was to meet me.

3 Without warning, a little girl ran out in front of the car, but I suddenly changed direction (___), and managed not to hit her.

4 It was so hot by the pool that, as she lay on her sunbed, she began to be half asleep (___).

5 He was made to feel sleepy (___) by the sound and movement of the train.

6 The Romans used ancient two-wheeled vehicles pulled by horses (___) for racing and for fighting.

7 The old farmer was riding a cart pulled by a pair of young castrated bulls (___).

8 As they entered the jungle clearing, they saw the ancient Aztec building used for the worship of gods (___) facing them.

9 Peter's thoughtful and serious behaviour (___) is rather unusual. After all, most youngsters his age are only interested in pop music and fashion.

10 The entrance to Tutankhamun's tomb was still <u>tightly closed</u> (___), showing that no grave robbers had broken in that way.

11 The monkey was sitting <u>with its shoulders up and its head down</u> (___) in the corner of its cage, looking sad, lonely, and bored.

12 Though he looked quite mature for his age, he still had the <u>high-pitched</u> (___) voice of a schoolboy.

13 If you train your dog when it's still young, it will always be <u>happy to follow orders</u> (___).

14 The house was <u>completely</u> (___) destroyed by the tornado.

15 He <u>used bad language</u> (___) when the paint tin fell on his foot.

---

a. awry /əˈraɪ/ (*adverb*)
b. bullocks /ˈbʊləks/ (*plural noun*)
c. chariots /ˈtʃærɪəts/ (*plural noun*)
d. drowse /draʊz/ (*infinitive verb*)
e. hunched up /hʌntʃt ˈʌp/ (*regular past tense multi-word verb*)
f. lulled /lʌld/ (*regular past tense verb*)
g. obedient /əˈbiːdɪənt/ (*adjective*)
h. piping /ˈpaɪpɪŋ/ (*adjective*)
i. sealed /siːld/ (*regular past tense verb used as adjective*)
j. sobriety /səˈbraɪətɪ/ (*noun*)
k. swerved /swɜːvd/ (*regular past tense verb*)
l. swore /swɔː/ (*irregular past tense verb*)
m. temple /ˈtempl/ (*noun*)
n. utterly /ˈʌtəlɪ/ (*adverb*)
o. vigorously /ˈvɪgərəslɪ/ (*adverb*)

Reading

1 Read the following extract from a short story called 'Old Man of the Temple' by RK Narayan. Answer the questions below. Give reasons for your answers.

a. What do you think the relationship between the two characters is?
b. Where do you think they are?
c. What do you think is wrong with Doss?
d. What do you think happened just before this conversation?
e. Why do you think the story is called 'Old Man of the Temple'?

Extract 1

*got down (Indian English) = got out (standard British English)

"DOSS, DOSS," I cried desperately. I got down*, walked to the front seat, opened the door, and shook him vigorously. He opened his eyes, assumed a hunched-up position, and rubbed his eyes with his hands, which trembled like an old man's.

"Do you feel better?" I asked. 5

"Better! Better! Hi! Hi!" he said in a thin, piping voice.

"What has happened to your voice? You sound like someone else," I said.

"Nothing. My voice is as good as it was. When a man is eighty he is bound to feel a few changes coming on." 10

"You aren't eighty, surely," I said.

"Not a day less," he said. "Is nobody going to move this vehicle? If not, there is no sense in sitting here all day. I will get down and go back to my temple."

"I don't know how to drive," I said. "And unless you do it, I don't see how 15 it can move."

"Me!" exclaimed Doss. "These new chariots! God knows what they are drawn by, I never understand, though I could handle a pair of bullocks in my time . . ."

2 Now read the beginning of the story. Were your guesses in **1** correct?

Extract 2

I HAD ENGAGED a taxi for going to Kumbum, which, as you may already know, is fifty miles from Malgudi. I went there one morning and it was past nine in the evening when I finished my business and started back for the town. Doss, the driver, was a young fellow of about twenty-five. He had often brought his car for me and I liked him. He was a well-behaved, 5 obedient fellow, with a capacity to sit and wait at the wheel, which is really a rare quality in a taxi driver. He drove the car smoothly, seldom swore at passers-by, and exhibited perfect judgment, good sense, and sobriety; and so I preferred him to any other driver whenever I had to go out on business.

It was about eleven when we passed the village Koopal, which is on the 10 way down. It was the dark half of the month and the surrounding country was swallowed up in the night. The village street was deserted. Everyone had gone to sleep; hardly any light was to be seen. The stars overhead sparkled brightly. Sitting in the back seat and listening to the continuous noise of the running wheels, I was half lulled into a drowse. 15

All of a sudden Doss swerved the car and shouted: "You old fool! Do you want to kill yourself?"

I was shaken out of my drowse and asked: "What is the matter?"

Doss stopped the car and said, "You see that old fellow, sir. He is trying to kill himself. I can't understand what he is up to." 20

I looked in the direction he pointed and asked, "Which old man?"

"There, there. He is coming towards us again. As soon as I saw him open

that temple door and come out I had a feeling, somehow, that I must keep an
eye on him.''

I took out my torch, got down, and walked about, but could see no one.   *25*
There was an old temple on the roadside. It was utterly in ruins; most por-
tions of it were mere mounds of old brick; the walls were awry; the doors
were shut to the main doorway, and brambles and thickets grew over and
covered them. It was difficult to guess with the aid of the torch alone what
temple it was and to what period it belonged.   *30*

"The doors are shut and sealed and don't look as if they had been opened
for centuries now," I cried.

"No, sir," Doss said coming nearer. "I saw the old man open the doors
and come out. He is standing there; shall we ask him to open them again if
you want to go in and see?"   *35*

I said to Doss, "Let us be going. We are wasting our time here."

We went back to the car. Doss sat in his seat, pressed the self-starter, and
asked without turning his head, "Are you permitting this fellow to come
with us, sir? He says he will get down at the next milestone."

"Which fellow?" I asked.   *40*

Doss indicated the space next to him.

"What is the matter with you, Doss? Have you had a drop of drink or
something?"

"I have never tasted any drink in my life, sir," he said, and added, "Get
down, old boy. Master says he can't take you."   *45*

"Are you talking to yourself?"

"After all, I think we needn't care for these unknown fellows on the road,"
he said.

"Doss," I pleaded. "Do you feel confident you can drive? If you feel dizzy
don't drive."   *50*

"Thank you, sir," said Doss. "I would rather not start the car now. I am
feeling a little out of sorts." I looked at him anxiously. He closed his eyes, his
breathing became heavy and noisy, and gradually his head sank.

**Comprehension
check**

1 Listen to Extract 2 and answer the following questions.

T.11a

a. What time of day was it when Doss and the narrator reached the village
   of Koopal?
b. Was the village busy?
c. Why did Doss swerve the car?
d. Why did the narrator get out of the car?
e. What was strange about the temple doors?
f. Why did the narrator ask if Doss had been drinking?
g. Why did Doss feel unwell?

2 The following are all true statements connected with the first two paragraphs in Extract 2. Look at lines 1–15 of Extract 2 again, and find the exact words and phrases which relate to each statement.

a. The narrator is from Malgudi.
b. The narrator was sitting in the back of the car.
c. Doss was regularly employed by the narrator.
d. It was difficult to see anything from the car.
e. Doss was a patient man.
f. The narrator had nearly fallen asleep in the car.
g. The narrator had been working until late on the day the story happened.
h. The narrator believed Doss to be a sensible person.

Looking at plot preparation

A good short story is economically written. Every piece of information given at the start is important in preparing for the main action which follows.

Work in groups. Why do you think the facts below are important in preparing for the scene of Doss's transformation? (You won't find the answers in the text!)

1 The narrator is from Malgudi.

Reason: _____

_____

2 The narrator believed Doss to be a sensible person.
Doss was regularly employed by the narrator.
Doss was a patient man.

Reason: _____

_____

3 The narrator was sitting in the back of the car.
It was difficult to see anything from the car.

Reason: _____

_____

4 The narrator had nearly fallen asleep in the car.
The narrator had been working until late on the day the story happened.

Reason: _____

_____

Points of style

There are several examples of Indian English in Extract 2. Below are their equivalents in standard British English. Find the original words that Narayan uses in the text, and the lines in which they appear.

Standard British English	Indian English	
1 got out (of a car)	got *down*	(line *28*)
2 will you allow . . . ?	_____	(line __)
3 I don't think we need worry about . . .	_____	(line __)
4 . . . engaged a taxi to go . . .	_____	(line __)
5 . . . on the way	_____	(line __)
6 . . . strangers . . .	_____	(line __)
7 . . . a capacity for sitting . . .	_____	(line __)

Listening

T.11b

Listen to Extract 1 as you read it again.

What do you think?

How do you think the story ends? Give reasons for your choice.

1 The spirit stays inside Doss, and he stops driving the taxi and goes to live in the temple.

2 The village priest wakes up and comes out of his house. He orders the spirit to leave Doss. With a terrible scream it does so.

3 The narrator tricks the spirit out of Doss by telling him that he is really dead, and by saying that his dead wife will come for him.

4 The narrator knocks Doss unconscious and walks to the nearest town, where he knows a psychologist who comes to help.

5 The spirit tells the narrator that there is some treasure hidden in the temple and then leaves Doss in peace.

> If you want to find out how the story by RK Narayan ends, read 'Old Man of the Temple' in the collection of short stories *Under the Banyan Tree*. You will also find the ending in the key at the back of this book.

12 A view of Christmas

CHARLES CAUSLEY *was born in 1917 in Cornwall, where he spent his youth. In 1940 he joined the Royal Navy and fought in the Second World War, after which he became a teacher and returned to Cornwall. His first poems were written as a result of his wartime experiences. 'Innocent's Song' was first published in the anthology* Johnny Alleluia *in 1961.*

What do you think?

The following words come from a modern poem. Check that you know what they all mean.

presents	smiling	children	carol
red	fireside	yellow	gingerbread
dancing	snow	white	Christmas

– What do you think the poem is about?
– What sort of atmosphere will the poem convey?
– What does the word 'Christmas' make you think of?
– Who are the traditional characters you think of at Christmas time?

Sentence completion

Underline the most appropriate words or phrases in italics to complete each of the following sentences.

1 Who's that knocking on the *door / window / ceiling?*

2 What are those presents lying *on the kitchen floor / under the tree / at the end of the bed?*

3 Who is the smiling *foreigner / visitor / stranger* with hair as white as *snow / gin / milk?*

4 Why has he got *snow / rubies / rings* on his fingers, and a *red hat / cold crown / bishop's mitre* on his head?

5 Why, when he *hums / caws / sings* his carol, does the *salty / white / cold* snow *melt / run red / fall?*

6 Why does he *sit by / stand by / ferry* my fireside *similar to / like / as an old friend / a spider on a thread / a poor beggar*?

7 His fingers are made of *fuses / biscuits / sausages*, and his tongue is made of *rubber / gingerbread / ham*.

8 Why does the world *melt in a million suns / continue to exist / go round* in front of him?

9 Why do his *yellow, yearning / blue, sparkling / brown, shining* eyes *twinkle like stars / glow like chocolate / burn like saffron buns*?

10 *See / Watch / Look* where he comes walking out of the Christmas *scene / flame / cold*.

11 He's dancing and *singing / double-talking / shouting*.

Reading and listening

1 Read and listen to the following poem by Charles Causley. Were your predictions in the sentence completion exercise above correct?

T.12

Innocent's Song

Who's that knocking on the window,
Who's that standing at the door,
What are all those presents
Lying on the kitchen floor?

Who is the smiling stranger   5
With hair as white as gin,
What is he doing with the children
And who could have let him in?

Why has he rubies on his fingers,
A cold, cold crown on his head,   10
Why, when he caws his carol,
Does the salty snow run red?

Why does he ferry my fireside
As a spider on a thread,
His fingers made of fuses   15
And his tongue of gingerbread?

Why does the world before him
Melt in a million suns,
Why do his yellow, yearning eyes
Burn like saffron buns?   20

Watch where he comes walking
Out of the Christmas flame,
Dancing, double-talking:

Herod is his name.

━0

2 Look back at the vocabulary box at the start of this unit. Are your general impressions the same now? What is the poem really about?

Note

When Jesus was born, Herod was King of Judea. He was visited in Jerusalem by three eastern astrologers looking for a new king. According to old prophecies Bethlehem was to be the birthplace of a great king, and Herod sent the wise men there, asking them to return and tell him where the child was so that he also could go and worship him. When the astrologers didn't return, Herod ordered his soldiers to find and kill all male children in Bethlehem of two years or under, hoping in this way to destroy the new king. In the Christian calendar 28 December is called Holy Innocent's Day in memory of the massacred children.

Comprehension check

Read the poem again and answer the following questions.

1 In lines 1–4 people are arriving at a house. Is the atmosphere relaxed or uneasy? What details make it so?

Which characters from the Herod story do you think the callers are?

   a. the dead children
   b. the three wise men
   c. Herod's soldiers

2 In lines 5–8 which traditional Christmas character does the stranger seem to be?

   a. one of the three wise men
   b. Father Christmas
   c. Saint Joseph

What does the description of his 'hair as white as gin' do to your overall impression of the stranger?

3 What do the rubies on his fingers (line 9) make you think of?

4 Why is the snow salty in line 12, do you think? And why is it red?

5 Lines 17–18 mention the world melting 'in a million suns'. What modern world disaster do you think is being referred to here?

6 Christmas is usually thought of as a cold time in England. What hot place is meant by the 'flame' Herod steps out of in line 22?

━0

Points of style

1 'Cawing' (line 11) is a harsh, croaking sound. Which of the following birds usually caws?

a *Dove*   b *Robin*   c *Raven*

What does this 'cawing' bird often symbolize?

2 Does the image of a spider moving to and fro in front of the fire suggest peace or restlessness?
What else does a spider on a thread suggest to you?
Why doesn't the poet use the word 'like' in line 14, do you think?

3 What associations do each of the following words have for you?

fingers _____

fuses _____

tongue _____

gingerbread _____

Does the putting together of 'fingers' and 'fuses' (line 15), and 'tongue' and 'gingerbread' (line 16) have a pleasant or unpleasant effect? Why?

4 Why is the word 'watch' used in line 21 instead of 'see' for example?

What do you think?

1 The poem has 24 lines. Is this important, do you think?
2 What would you say is the general message of the poem?

Writing

Choose an evil character out of literature, myth, or history. (It can be one of those below, or someone of your own choice.) Write a poem or a piece of prose describing your chosen character in an unexpected way.

Lady Macbeth	Adolf Hitler	Faust
Genghis Khan	Bluebeard	Salome
Caligula	Lucrezia Borgia	Joseph Stalin

13 What's in a name?

OSCAR WILDE *was born in 1854 in Dublin where he lived and was educated until he went to Magdalen College, Oxford, to continue his studies. He became famous for his writing from the 1880s onwards, and was equally talented as a dramatist, novelist, short story writer, essayist, and poet. In 1895, when he was at the height of his success, Wilde was sent to prison. After his release in 1897, he left Britain and went to live abroad. Wilde died in Paris in 1900.* The Importance of Being Earnest *was first performed at the St. James' Theatre in London in 1895, and was published in 1899.*

Discussion

Read and discuss the quotations below.

> **What's in a name? That which we call a rose**
> **By any other name would smell as sweet.**
>
> WILLIAM SHAKESPEARE (1564–1616) *Poet and dramatist*

> *Father calls me William, sister calls me Will,*
> *Mother calls me Willie, but the fellers call me Bill!*
>
> EUGENE FIELD (1850–1895) *Poet and humorist*

> *I think it humanly impossible for anyone to think of his own name as a word of little importance.*
>
> FRANK CASE (1870–1946) *Hotel-keeper and author*

> **PEOPLE IF YOU LIKE TO BELIEVE IT CAN BE MADE BY THEIR NAMES. CALL ANYBODY PAUL AND THEY GET TO BE A PAUL CALL ANYBODY ALICE AND THEY GET TO BE AN ALICE PERHAPS YES PERHAPS NO ...**
>
> GERTRUDE STEIN (1874–1946) *Literary experimenter*

Work in pairs. Interview each other using the following questions.

- What name(s) did your parents give you? Was there any special reason for their choice?
- Do different people call you by different names? If so, what names do they use and why? Which do you most like being called, and which least?
- Have you ever changed your name? If so, when and why?
- Would you like to change your name? If so, what would you change it to and why?
- What is your favourite name for a girl? And for a boy? Why do you like these names?
- Are there any names you hate? Why? How would you feel if you met someone with one of these names?
- When do you find it easy and when do you find it difficult to remember names?

Vocabulary

First read the following fifteen sentences, concentrating on the underlined words. Then use the sentences to help you match a word in **A** with a definition in **B**.

She sent the <u>manuscript</u> of her first novel to twenty-six publishers, and it was rejected by every one.

My parents lived in India when I was young so I was looked after in England by my <u>guardian</u>.

Most of the local community centre's money comes from gifts from <u>charitable</u> men and women in the neighbourhood.

My grandmother lent me an old-fashioned <u>perambulator</u> when my daughter was born. We used to take her to the park in it.

Many of the more <u>remote</u> mountain villages are completely cut off by snow in the winter.

Using red hot irons, the cowboys <u>branded</u> the cows one by one, burning a big letter 'S' – for Southwood Ranch – on each one's back.

We experienced one <u>misfortune</u> after another: my bag got lost on the flight, Caroline's passport was stolen soon after we arrived, and we both got food poisoning.

The two sisters, who hadn't seen each other for many years, <u>embraced</u> warmly when they met again.

<u>Canon</u> Woods spoke about raising £5,000 to have the great organ repaired.

She is an <u>earnest</u>, intellectual-looking young woman, and a good student.

The old house had <u>capacious</u> fitted cupboards, so we didn't have to buy any wardrobes.

Her teachers recommended that she see a psychiatrist on account of her difficult <u>disposition</u>.

'The best things come in small packages,' as my <u>late</u> grandmother – a rather short woman – used to say.

He was filled with <u>shame</u> when his new girlfriend discovered that he worked in a garage and wasn't a professional pop star at all.

That painting of a dog sitting sadly by his dead master's tomb is a perfect example of 19th century <u>sentimentality</u>.

A	B
1 manuscript /ˈmænjəskrɪpt/ (n)	a. something extremely undesirable that happens to you
2 guardian /ˈgɑːdjən/ (n)	b. uncomfortable feeling you get when you have done something wrong
3 charitable /ˈtʃærətəbl/ (adj)	c. the way someone behaves or feels (formal)
4 perambulator /pəˈræmbjʊleɪtə/ (n)	d. legal protector
5 remote /rɪˈməʊt/ (adj)	e. to take someone into one's arms, to hug (formal)
6 brand /brænd/ (v)	f. baby carriage, pram (archaic or very formal)
7 misfortune /mɪsˈfɔːtʃuːn/ (n)	g. handwritten or typed version of a book before it is printed
8 embrace /ɪmˈbreɪs/ (v)	h. to mark something permanently
9 canon /ˈkænən/ (n)	i. able to contain a lot, roomy (very formal)
10 earnest /ˈɜːnɪst/ (adj)	j. far from – in distance or time
11 capacious /kəˈpeɪʃəs/ (adj)	k. exaggerated emotional style – over-sad or over-romantic
12 disposition /dɪspəˈzɪʃn/ (n)	l. no longer living – used especially of someone who has recently died
13 late /leɪt/ (adj)	m. kindly, generous
14 shame /ʃeɪm/ (n)	n. serious
15 sentimentality /sentɪmenˈtæləti/ (n)	o. a clergyman who is part of the staff of a cathedral

Reading and discussion

1 Work in three groups. You are going to read three extracts from *The Importance of Being Earnest*, a play by Oscar Wilde. Each group will read a different extract.

While you read, try to answer the following questions:

a. Who are the characters?
b. What is the relationship between them?
c. What is happening in your extract?
d. What do you think happened before your extract?
e. What do you think will happen after your extract?

Group A   Read Extract A on page 80.
Group B   Read Extract B on page 83.
Group C   Read extract C on page 96.

2 Stay in your group and compare your answers.

3 Now get into groups of three: one A student, one B student, and one C student.

Without showing the other two students the extract you have just read, tell them about it.

Listen carefully as the other two students describe their extracts. (You may want to reconsider your answers to some of the questions in 1 when you hear what they say.)

4 Decide which extract comes near the beginning, which in the middle, and which near the end of the play.

> The best way to check your answers would be to read the whole play. There is also a 1952 film version of the play available on video in Britain, so you may want to watch this instead. If you are unable to do either of these, there is a plot summary in the answer key.

What do you think?

Why do you think the play is called *The Importance of Being Earnest: A Trivial Comedy for Serious People*?

Listening

T.13

Listen to the three extracts in the order they occur in the play. Which is your favourite character? Why?

Discussion

Look at these photographs of a 1909 production of the play. Use the names in the centre to identify the characters. What do you think is happening in each scene?

In the Town

In the Country

Algernon ☐
Lady Bracknell ☐
Cecily ☐
Dr Chasuble ☐
Ernest (×2) ☐ ☐
Gwendolen ☐
Jack ☐
Miss Prism ☐

Project work

The pictures below show some important people and events connected with Oscar Wilde. 'The Oscar Wilde Story' is an interesting one. Find out as much as you can about Oscar Wilde's life. How was it influenced by Victorian values?

After finding out about Oscar Wilde's life, read *The Importance of Being Earnest* again. Does the play mean any more to you now that you know some more about the author?

14 Goodbye love

WILLIAM SHAKESPEARE *was born in Stratford-upon-Avon in 1564. At the age of eighteen he married Anne Hathaway, of Shottery, a village close to Stratford. She was eight years older than Shakespeare. In 1592 he appeared as an actor and playwright in London and was an immediate success. In 1599 he bought a share in the newly-built Globe Theatre in London where many of his plays were performed. He wrote at least thirty-seven plays: comedies, tragedies, and histories. His sonnet sequence was first published in 1609. The Globe Theatre burned down in 1613 and Shakespeare retired to Stratford at about that time. He died in 1616.*

What do you think? **1** Work on your own. What do the following things make you think of? Write five adjectives, nouns, or verbs connected with each subject in the grid below.

Autumn	Dusk	A fire going out	The end of a relationship

2 Now get into groups of three. Compare the lists of words you have each made. Discuss and make a note of any differences.

**Reading and
listening**

1   Can you find any of the words that you listed in the four paragraphs below?

YOU CAN see that time of year in me when it's cold and there are few yellow
leaves, or none at all on the branches of the trees. Not so long
ago the birds sang sweetly in those branches, but now they're bare, like empty
choir stalls in a ruined church.

You can see the half-light of dusk in me, after the sun has set in the west. Gradually the light fades, the day is over, and night comes on, like a copy of death,
closing everything up and bringing peace.

You can see a fire in me; a fire which is glowing in the ashes, like an old man
lying on his deathbed, shortly to die, a shadow of his former youthful self; a fire
which has been eaten up by the thing that once fed it.

You notice these things, and that makes your love stronger, so that you give a
lot of love to what you will leave in the near future.

The passage you have just read is a modern prose version of a fourteen-line
poem, or 'sonnet', by William Shakespeare. Shakespeare's Sonnets were
published in 1609.

2   Below are Shakespeare's original words. Using the modern version above to
help you, put the couplets into the correct order.

a. As the deathbed whereon it must expire,
    Consum'd with that which it was nourish'd by.

b. That time of year thou mayst in me behold
    When yellow leaves, or none, or few, do hang

c. This thou perceiv'st, which makes thy love more strong,
    To love that well which thou must leave ere long.

d. Which by-and-by black night doth take away,
    Death's second self, that seals up all in rest.

e. Upon those boughs which shake against the cold,
    Bare ruin'd choirs where late the sweet birds sang.

f. In me thou see'st the glowing of such fire
    That on the ashes of his youth doth lie,

g. In me thou see'st the twilight of such day
    As after sunset fadeth in the West,

T.14

3 Listen and read the sonnet below to check your answer.

Sonnet LXXIII

That time of year thou mayst in me behold
  When yellow leaves, or none, or few, do hang
Upon those boughs which shake against the cold,
  Bare ruin'd choirs where late the sweet birds sang.
In me thou see'st the twilight of such day
  As after sunset fadeth in the West,
Which by-and-by black night doth take away,
  Death's second self, that seals up all in rest.
In me thou see'st the glowing of such fire
  That on the ashes of his youth doth lie,
As the deathbed whereon it must expire,
  Consum'd with that which it was nourish'd by.
    This thou perceiv'st, which makes thy
      love more strong,
    To love that well which thou must
      leave ere long.

Note

In Shakespeare's time, some grammar and spelling rules were different from those used today:

Present Simple second person singular verbs ended in -est, -'st, or -st.

Present Simple third person singular verbs ended in -eth, -th, or -s.

Spelling matched pronunciation. Words ending in -ed, for example, were said with /ed/ at the end. (This is why *see'st*, *ruin'd*, *consum'd*, *nourish'd*, and *perceiv'st* have an apostrophe – to show a silent 'e'.)

Vocabulary

Shakespeare's English contains some words which are either archaic or poetic. Can you match up the following archaic/poetic words with their modern English equivalents in the box below?

1 thou _____   5 doth _____

2 behold _____   6 whereon _____

3 boughs _____   7 thy _____

4 his _____   8 ere _____

branches	on which	before	its
does	you (*singular*)	your (*singular*)	see

Comprehension check

Read the sonnet again and look at the statements below. Decide if they are true (T), or false (F). Correct the false statements.

1 The poem is about the end of a love affair.

2 In the poem Shakespeare compares his lover to autumn, dusk, and a dying fire.

3 Shakespeare has noticed that his lover seems to love him less now than before.

4 Shakespeare feels that his lover will leave him soon.

5 The mood of the poem is sad and nostalgic.

Points of style

The poem contains many rich images. Look at the following unfinished sentences. Tick (✓) the completion which best explains the image each time. (Sometimes more than one completion is possible.)

1 The phrase 'shake against the cold' (line 3) gives the idea of ...

  a. the naked trees shivering in the autumn wind.
  b. someone shaking their fist angrily at the approaching winter.
  c. someone shaking violently with an illness.

2 The comparison of the autumn branches with 'bare ruin'd choirs' (line 4) works because ...

  a. branches are of living wood, whereas choirstalls are made of dead wood.
  b. autumn trees look like the pillars of a ruined church which is open to the sky.
  c. birds often sit on branches in rows – like choirboys in choirstalls.

3 The 'sweet birds' which sang in the trees (line 4) represent . . .

    a. the carefree happiness of musicians.
    b. the carefree happiness of youth.
    c. the carefree happiness of summer.

4 By saying that he was once 'nourish'd' but is now 'consum'd' by love (line 12), Shakespeare means . . .

    a. love was once a strengthening and enjoyable thing for him, like eating.
    b. the lack of love he now feels is like being starved.
    c. he is now being weakened and destroyed by love, like someone being eaten up by a disease.

5 The three images of autumn, dusk, and a dying fire work well together in the poem because . . .

    a. they are variations on the same theme of things ending, dying, and getting darker.
    b. they all suggest warm colours, like yellow, orange, and red.
    c. they are all very different, and make an unexpected combination.

What do you think?

Do you agree with the following statements about the poem? If not, what do you think?

1 Some writers have criticized Shakespeare for writing quickly and not revising his work.

". . . in his writing (whatsoever he penned) he never blotted out a line."
Ben Jonson (1572–1637) Dramatist and poet

"Shakespeare never had six lines together without a fault."
Samuel Johnson (1709–84) Poet, critic, and essayist

In line 2, a more usual sentence construction would be:

When yellow leaves, <u>and few, or none,</u> do hang
Upon those boughs . . .

Shakespeare probably used an unusual phrase order here because of the speed and carelessness of his writing.

2 Line 2 could have been written with a full stop at the end:

When yellow leaves upon those boughs do hang.

Instead the verb *hang upon* is divided between lines 2 and 3 to emphasize the fact that some last leaves are still hanging from the branches.

3 Shakespeare includes repeated 's' sounds in line 8 to suggest the whistling of the wind in the trees.

4 The opposite of *love* is usually *hate*, but the opposite of *love* in this poem is *leave*.

Writing

Write a short poem describing either a parting between two people, or the end of a relationship in your life. Use the adjectives, nouns, and verbs you collected in the grid at the beginning of the unit. Your poem need not rhyme, but you can use repeated consonant sounds if you want.

> If you have enjoyed reading this sonnet by Shakespeare, you may want to find a translation of sonnet 73 into your own language. Having studied the sonnet in some detail in English, you should be able to examine the translation critically, noting the similarities and differences in style and content between the original and the translated version. If you can find two different translations of the same sonnet, you may find it interesting to compare them, deciding which is more faithful to the original, and which you prefer.

Extract A

Unit 13 ## What's in a name?

[*Enter* JACK.]

GWENDOLEN [*Catching sight of him.*] Ernest! My own Ernest!

JACK Gwendolen! Darling! [*Offers to kiss her.*]

GWENDOLEN [*Drawing back.*] A moment! May I ask if you are engaged to be married to this young lady? [*Points to* CECILY.]

JACK [*Laughing.*] To dear little Cecily! Of course not! What could have put such an idea into your pretty little head?

GWENDOLEN Thank you. You may! [*Offers her cheek.*]

CECILY [*Very sweetly.*] I knew there must be some misunderstanding, Miss Fairfax. The gentleman whose arm is at present round your waist is my guardian, Mr. John Worthing.

GWENDOLEN I beg your pardon?

CECILY This is Uncle Jack.

GWENDOLEN [*Receding.*] Jack! Oh!
[*Enter* ALGERNON.]

CECILY Here is Ernest.

ALGERNON [*Goes straight over to* CECILY *without noticing any one else.*] My own love! [*Offers to kiss her.*]

CECILY [*Drawing back.*] A moment, Ernest! May I ask you – are you engaged to be married to this young lady?

ALGERNON [*Looking round.*] To what young lady? Good heavens! Gwendolen!

CECILY Yes! to good heavens, Gwendolen, I mean to Gwendolen.

ALGERNON [*Laughing.*] Of course not! What could have put such an idea into your pretty little head?

CECILY Thank you. [*Presenting her cheek to be kissed.*] You may. [ALGERNON *kisses her.*]

GWENDOLEN I felt there was some slight error, Miss Cardew. The gentleman who is now embracing you is my cousin, Mr. Algernon Moncrieff.

CECILY [*Breaking away from* ALGERNON.] Algernon Moncrieff! Oh! [*The two girls move towards each other and put their arms round each other's waists as if for protection.*]

Pronunciation note
Gwendolen = /ˈgwendəlɪn/
Algernon = /ˈældʒənən/

Tapescript section

MATILDA

Matilda told such Dreadful Lies,
It made one Gasp and Stretch one's Eyes;
Her Aunt, who, from her Earliest Youth,
Had kept a Strict Regard for Truth,
Attempted to Believe Matilda:
The effort very nearly killed her,
And would have done so, had not She
Discovered this Infirmity.
For once, towards the Close of Day,
Matilda, growing tired of play,
And finding she was left alone,
Went tiptoe to the Telephone
And summoned the Immediate Aid
Of London's Noble Fire-Brigade.
Within an hour the Gallant Band
Were pouring in on every hand,
From Putney, Hackney Downs and Bow,
With Courage high and Hearts a-glow
They galloped, roaring through the Town,
'Matilda's House is Burning Down!'
Inspired by British Cheers and Loud
Proceeding from the Frenzied Crowd,
They ran their ladders through a score
Of windows on the Ball Room Floor;
And took Peculiar Pains to Souse
The Pictures up and down the House,
Until Matilda's Aunt succeeded
In showing them they were not needed
And even then she had to pay
To get the Men to go away!

It happened that a few Weeks later
Her Aunt was off to the Theatre
To see that Interesting Play

The Second Mrs Tanqueray.
She had refused to take her Niece
To hear this Entertaining Piece:
A Deprivation Just and Wise
To Punish her for Telling Lies.
That Night a Fire *did* break out –
You should have heard Matilda Shout!
You should have heard her Scream and Bawl,
And throw the window up and call
To People passing in the Street –
(The rapidly increasing Heat
Encouraging her to obtain
Their confidence) – but all in vain!
For every time she shouted 'Fire!'
They only answered 'Little Liar!'
And therefore when her Aunt returned,
Matilda, and the House, were Burned.

Unit 7

Tapescript 7

THE RIVER GOD
(of the River Mimram in Hertfordshire)

I may be smelly and I may be old,
Rough in my pebbles, reedy in my pools,
But where my fish float by I bless their swimming
And I like the people to bathe in me, especially women.
But I can drown the fools
Who bathe too close to the weir, contrary to rules.
And they take a long time drowning
As I throw them up now and then in a spirit of clowning.
Hi yih, yippity-yap, merrily I flow,
O I may be an old foul river but I have plenty of go.
Once there was a lady who was too bold
She bathed in me by the tall black cliff where the water runs
    cold,
So I brought her down here
To be my beautiful dear.
Oh will she stay with me will she stay
This beautiful lady, or will she go away?
She lies in my beautiful deep river bed with many a weed
To hold her, and many a waving reed.
Oh who would guess what a beautiful white face lies there
Waiting for me to smooth and wash away the fear
She looks at me with. Hi yih, do not let her
Go. There is no one on earth who does not forget her
Now. They say I am a foolish old smelly river
But they do not know of my wide original bed
Where the lady waits, with her golden sleepy head.
If she wishes to go I will not forgive her.

Extract B

What's in a name?

LADY BRACKNELL [*In a severe, judicial voice.*] Prism! [MISS PRISM *bows her head in shame.*] Come here, Prism! [MISS PRISM *approaches in a humble manner.*] Prism! Where is that baby? [*General consternation. The* CANON *starts back in horror.* ALGERNON *and* JACK *pretend to be anxious to shield* CECILY *and* GWENDOLEN *from hearing the details of a terrible public scandal.*] Twenty-eight years ago, Prism, you left Lord Bracknell's house, Number 104, Upper Grosvenor Street, in charge of a perambulator that contained a baby of the male sex. You never returned. A few weeks later, through the elaborate investigations of the Metropolitan police, the perambulator was discovered at midnight, standing by itself in a remote corner of Bayswater. It contained the manuscript of a three-volume novel of more than usually revolting sentimentality. [MISS PRISM *starts in involuntary indignation.*] But the baby was not there! [*Every one looks at* MISS PRISM.] Prism! Where is that baby? [*A pause.*]

MISS PRISM Lady Bracknell, I admit with shame that I do not know. I only wish I did. The plain facts of the case are these. On the morning of the day you mention, a day that is for ever branded on my memory, I prepared as usual to take the baby out in its perambulator. I had also with me a somewhat old, but capacious hand-bag in which I had intended to place the manuscript of a work of fiction that I had written during my few unoccupied hours. In a moment of mental abstraction, for which I never can forgive myself, I deposited the manuscript in the basinette*, and placed the baby in the hand-bag.

*basinette – perambulator

JACK [*Who has been listening attentively.*] But where did you deposit the hand-bag?

MISS PRISM Do not ask me, Mr. Worthing.

JACK Miss Prism, this is a matter of no small importance to me. I insist on knowing where you deposited the hand-bag that contained that infant.

MISS PRISM I left it in the cloak-room of one of the larger railway stations in London.

JACK What railway station?

MISS PRISM [*Quite crushed.*] Victoria. The Brighton line. [*Sinks into a chair.*]

JACK I must retire to my room for a moment. Gwendolen, wait here for me.

GWENDOLEN If you are not too long, I will wait here for you all my life. [*Exit* JACK *in great excitement.*]

Pronunciation note
Gwendolen = /ˈgwendəlɪn/
Algernon = /ˈældʒənən/

Answer key

Introductory unit

Vocabulary of literature

Prose	Poetry	Drama
anthology	anthology	anthology
author	author	author
chapter	character	character
character	description	comedy
description	dialogue	description
dialogue	narration	dialogue
essayist	poet	dramatist
fiction	point of view	playwright
narration	pseudonym	plot
non-fiction	rhyme	pseudonym
novelist	setting	scene
paragraph	stanza	script
plot	verse	setting
point of view		stage directions
pseudonym		tragedy
setting		whodunnit
whodunnit		

Unit 1   Trouble at school

Vocabulary

2 i.	4 a.	6 k.	8 f.	10 j.
3 d.	5 c.	7 b.	9 g.	11 h.

Reading

The title that best summarizes the passage is 3 Capture.

Comprehension check

1 The headmaster at the boys' school.
2 The owner of a sweet shop where the boys played a trick.
3 One of the boys who played the trick. A friend of the author.
4 (Not in the passage) Roald Dahl. He is writing about himself as a child.
5 A sweet shop.
6 No. Mr Coombes seems slightly embarrassed by Mrs Pratchett. She seems to respect him.
7 (Not in the passage) He is eight.
8 They put a dead mouse in a jar of sweets in Mrs Pratchett's shop.
9 He was going to punish them.
10 They are going to be punished by Mr Coombes.
11 She has piggy little eyes and dirty fingers.
12 In the school playground.
13 (Not in the passage) After Assembly in the morning.
14 (Not in the passage) A Church school.
15 They are in an identity parade so Mrs Pratchett can identify the guilty boys.

Points of style

1   **General structure**

a. Mrs Pratchett is presented as speaking a variety of English with the following differences from standard British English:
   – Third person singular extended to third person plural (e.g. 'they comes into my shop') and to first person singular (e.g. 'I never forgets a face').
   – Her pronunciation is represented in written form as if she drops the *h*'s from the beginning of words (e.g. ''im' for him, ''eadmaster' for headmaster).

b. She is portrayed as being lower class in this way.

c. The use of direct speech to portray dialogue does two things:
   – It makes the passage more immediate, although it is set in the past.
   – It presents the conversation as objective fact rather than as an event from memory. It is, of course, unlikely that Dahl would have any memory at all of the actual words spoken.

d. The sentences are generally short. Grammatical structure is simple with few embedded phrases and clauses. Because of this the passage reads as if Roald Dahl were still a boy writing about his experiences.

2 **Slang vocabulary**
b. 1 nasty (line 3)
2 cheeky (line 3)
3 nick (line 7)
4 grubby (line 8), scummy (line 16)
5 bounder (line 16)
6 stinking (line 39)

Unit 2   A housewife speaks

Reading 1

– The text is by a housewife.
– It's about morning routines and family life.
– The mood is optimistic in the first paragraph and realistic in the second paragraph.

Comprehension check

1 The woman usually gets up late, prepares breakfast and quarrels with her husband. She sends her children off to school, and her husband off to work. Then she does the washing up.

2 Her children usually go to school dressed untidily. Her husband usually goes to work in a bad mood, after a noisy and argumentative breakfast.

3 The woman described in lines 3–4 is the perfect housewife. It is not a realistic picture.

4 The children only kicked the cat enough to make it lose its dignity, not enough to injure it. They calmed the cat down afterwards before they went off to school.

5 The woman's husband earned the insults. The woman aimed them. The insults are described as having barbs, because they are sharp and painful and, like fish hooks, now that they are under his skin, they are difficult to get out again.

6 On the surface everything may seem all right by tonight, but we imagine that tomorrow won't really be any different.

Reading 2

1 When written as a poem, the text seems funnier and a bit less depressing.

2 The fact that the whole poem is built up of curves suggests a female body. Looking at the poem in this way, we can see the title as hair, line 14 as the waist, lines 15–24 as the woman's skirt and lines 25–27 as her ankles and feet.

3 The curve of the title 'Resolution' suggests a resolution which starts strongly and gets weaker.

The curves of line 5 'organize the children' could suggest someone picking up two children.

The curve of line 10 'lowered' helps the description of lowered eyelids.

The curve of line 14 'middle' helps the description of parted hair.

The capital letters in line 15 'SHOUTING IS OVER AND' help to give the idea of shouting.

The layout of lines 25–27 'Tomorrow/will be/ different' is exactly the same as that of line 1–3, which reinforces the message and rounds off the poem.

Unit 3   Whodunnit

Reading

– The most important difference is that Johnnie is on the terrace with his father and not in the car.
– Johnnie is dark-haired, not flaxen.
– The time on the grandfather clock in the council chamber is 4 o'clock, not 12.10.
– There is only one policeman with the tramp instead of two.
– The car is black and has only one person in it.

Comprehension check

1 a. Johnnie was driven away in a car.
b. Poirot was interested in the case.
c. The constable caught a man.
d. The man intended to drug and kidnap Johnnie.
e. Inspector McNeil was in charge of the case.
f. Mrs Waverly was worried about Johnnie.
g. Mr Waverly forgot to take Johnnie outside.

h. A note was found on the man.

i. The grandfather clock had been put forward 10 minutes.

2   Order: e, c, d, h, a, g, i, b, f.

Vocabulary

1 a.	4 a.	7 c.	10 c.	13 c.
2 b.	5 c.	8 a.	11 c.	14 a.
3 a.	6 c.	9 b.	12 b.	15 b.

What do you think? – Summary

The Waverlys are an important English family. Their money comes from Mrs Waverly's father, and she is not generous with it. This causes problems for her husband who enjoys the pleasures of life.

Mr Waverly plans the kidnapping of their child as a way to get some of his wife's money. He writes the notes before the kidnapping and changes the clock. He secretly gives his wife a small amount of poison, which makes her ill, so that she has to stay in bed. This 'mysterious poisoning' also gives him a good reason for sending away most of the servants, except for the butler and housekeeper. He hires the man to deliver the package to the house at 11.50, then hides Johnnie in a secret room when everyone runs onto the terrace. Later he moves him to another hiding place with his old nurse.

The man in the car is a friend of Mr Waverly's who picks up a young fair-haired boy in the village and drives through the garden with him at the appointed time. Tredwell is loyal to Mr Waverly and dislikes Mrs Waverly. He hired the man in the garden to deliver the package on Mr Waverly's orders.

Poirot solves the crime. He confronts Mr Waverly with his knowledge, and makes him promise to return his son the following day. He tells no one else in order to avoid any scandal, because the Waverlys, and not the police, hired him.

Poirot solves the crime using the following clues:
– The clock must have been changed by someone in the house.
– It would have been easier for an outsider to kidnap the boy without giving a warning.
– The man caught in the garden insists that he was hired by Tredwell.
– Mr Waverly defends Tredwell absolutely.
– The personalities of Mr and Mrs Waverly.
– The footprint of a toy dog in the dust in the secret room.

Unit 4   Never tell a lie

Vocabulary

1			
	b. infirmity		e. succeeded
	c. entertaining		f. confidence
	d. deprivation		g. dreadful

2			
	b. peculiar		g. gallant
	c. aid		h. band
	d. noble		i. pains
	e. bawl		j. souse
	f. just		

Listening

2				
	line 3	Youth	line 31	later
	line 10	play	line 33	Play
	line 12	Telephone	line 35	Niece
	line 14	Fire-Brigade	line 38	Lies
	line 19	Town	line 39	out
	line 24	Floor	line 42	call
	line 26	House	line 43	Street
	line 28	needed	line 48	Liar
	line 29	pay	line 50	Burned

Comprehension check

1   a. Matilda is a liar.

b. She calls the fire brigade at the start of the poem because she is bored with just playing.

c. When they arrive, the firemen break the windows on the ballroom floor with their ladders, and soak the paintings throughout the house with the water from their hoses.

d. Matilda's aunt gets them to go away by paying them.

e. Matilda doesn't go with her aunt to the theatre because she has to stay at home, as a punishment for telling lies.

f. Nobody helps Matilda when she asks for help at the end of the poem. They don't believe her this time because they know that she has a habit of telling lies.

2   a. To 'caution' means to warn, and 'verse' is another name for rhymed poetry. The title suggests that the poem has a warning message that should be taken seriously. A 'Cautionary Tale' is a story which

presents a general rule for good behaviour, and gives an example of what may happen if the rule is not followed. (A 'story with a moral' is a more modern name for this.)

b. Belloc probably intended the poem to be read aloud by parents to their children.

c. The poem is funny. When we were children we learnt 'Matilda' by heart because we liked it so much. We found the dreadful ending powerful, however, and took the moral seriously.

d. (possible answer) If you tell lies something terrible may happen to you.

e. Matilda/killed her – lines 5–6
had not she/Infirmity – lines 7–8
later/Theatre – lines 31–32
The forced rhymes are unexpected and very funny.

f. Many nouns and some other words start, unusually, with capital letters to show that they should be strongly stressed when the verse is read.
This use of capital letters to emphasize words is another way in which Belloc adds humour to the poem. This humour, though, is probably only noticed by adults.

Unit 5   Punishment and control

Vocabulary

a. **Criminal**
b. **Crime**
c. cell
d. **Rules**
e. uniform
f. courtyard
g. roll call
h. beating
i. **Punishment**

Comprehension check

1   a. T (lines 2–3 tell us this)

b. Don't know (line 4 tells us that there is roll call three times a day, but not exactly when)

c. F (lines 11–12 tell us that the boys were beaten in the past, but not any more)

d. T (line 14 tells us this)

e. F (line 17 tells us that although the boys think that being put in a cell alone is better for them, they actually preferred the beatings)

f. Don't know (line 19 tells us that 'speaking when you shouldn't' is against the school rules, but we don't know exactly when the silent periods are)

g. F (lines 19–20 list three very petty rules)

h. T (lines 21–23 tell us this)

i. F (line 25 tells us the boys like to follow the school rules)

j. Don't know (line 31 tells us the boys must get undressed before getting into bed, but not exactly what they do or do not wear in bed)

k. T (lines 34–35 tell us this)

l. T (lines 40–43 tell us this)

Vocabulary 2 and listening

2   New boy: aggressive, rebellious, and inquisitive
Old boys: docile, mesmerized, brainwashed, conformist, cowed, and credulous

Unit 6   Choosing a career

Vocabulary

2   a. eavesdropped
b. lap
c. nodded
d. squalor
e. perplexed
f. kindled
g. whim
h. depraved
i. resolve
j. pitfalls
k. deliberation

Reading 1

1   a. Masuji says nothing about wanting to be a professional artist. He listens to his father in silence.

b. Masuji's father does not approve of his plans. He says he will be ashamed if his son becomes an artist, and then tells the boy to leave the room.

c. Sachiko has told her husband about Masuji's wish to be a professional artist. This is why he wants to talk to Masuji. At the beginning of the meeting she tries to make excuses for her son, and to reconcile Masuji and his father, but in the end she agrees with her husband.

Reading 2

1 a. Masuji's father burns his paintings to stop him from becoming an artist.

   b. Masuji's mother does nothing to stop her husband. When she meets her son in the dark corridor, she pretends she does not know what her husband is doing, and says he is working on something.

   c. Masuji doesn't give up his plans because of what his parents do. Instead he becomes more determined than before to become an artist.

Unit 7   The tale of a river

Vocabulary

1 b. reed   f. drown   j. fear
   c. bless   g. bold   k. clowning
   d. bathe   h. weed   l. flow
   e. weir   i. float

2 b. foul   e. plenty of go
   c. merrily   f. cliff
   d. contrary to   g. bed

Listening

1 line 1   old   line 16   go
   line 3   float   line 18   hold
   line 6   close   line 19   Oh
   line 8   throw   line 22   Go . . . no
   line 9   flow   line 23   old
   line 10   O* . . . old . . . go   line 24   know
   line 11   bold   line 25   golden
   line 12   cold   line 26   go
   line 15   Oh

   *poetic spelling of Oh

2 a. They all contain the sound /əʊ/.
   b. The repetition of these vowel sounds in the poem suggests the repetitive sound of water flowing, or of the River God's sighs.

Comprehension check

1 (possible answers)
   (a) River God/river
   (b) women
   (c) drowns/kills
   (d) weir

   (e) swam/bathed/went/was swimming/was bathing
   (f) river bed/bottom of the river
   (g) prisoner/wife/girlfriend/lover/beautiful dear
   (h) afraid/frightened/terrified
   (i) leave/abandon
   (j) foolish
   (k) old
   (l) smelly
   (m) waiting

2 a. Line 2 plays with the expression 'rough and ready'.

   b. The nonsense words 'Hi yih, yippity-yap' and 'Hi yih' give the impression that the River God is a wild, foolish, animal thing, full of energy.

   c. the weir

   d. The word 'bed' in line 17 means river bed, marriage bed, and death bed.

   e. According to lines 22/23 the woman has been under the river for a long time, since no one now remembers her.

   f. River God: smelly, old, rough, reedy, foul, foolish
      Lady: bold, beautiful, white, golden

   g. The River God loves the woman because she is his opposite. She is adventurous, attractive, and desirable. He is ugly, old, smelly, and stupid.

   h. The phrase 'wide original bed' in line 24 suggests the river has been spoilt by people, who have built the weir to control it, and have probably put rubbish in it. Now it is narrow and smelly as a result. In its original, natural state it was wide and fresh, and the River God looks back to this unspoilt time, which modern people do not know of, with nostalgia.

Points of style

1 a. old (line 1) is repeated twice (in lines 10 and 23)
   b. smelly (line 1) is repeated once (in line 23)
   c. beautiful (line 14) is repeated three times (in lines 16, 17, and 19)
   d. lady (line 11) is repeated twice (in lines 16 and 25)

2 a. bathed (line 12)
   b. reed (line 18)
   c. drowning (line 7)
   d. foolish (line 23)
   e. waits (line 25)

3 rough *in my* pebbles, reedy *in my* pools (line 2)
will she stay with me *will she stay* . . . or *will she* go away? (lines 15–16)
many a weed / To hold her, and *many a* waving reed (lines 17–18)
Like a river which gets bigger and stronger as it flows on, each time a word is repeated it becomes more powerful. The repetitions and near repetitions also suggest the noise made by a river, which is repetitive but never exactly the same from one minute to the next.

4 a. lines 11 and 12 rhyme with line 1
  b. lines 5 and 6 rhyme with line 2
  c. lines 13 and 14 rhyme with line 20 (and line 19 half rhymes with it)

The pattern of the rhymes – mainly rhyming couplets, but with some odd lines that link with earlier or later couplets – gives the idea of the patterns made by river water, moving back on itself in circles, dividing and meeting, as it flows onwards.

Unit 8 New buildings and old

Vocabulary 1

2 e.   4 f.   6 a.   8 i.   10 g.
3 d.   5 c.   7 h.   9 k.   11 j.

Reading 1

1 a. A fat, middle-aged woman, a chairman, and another man are speaking.
   b. They are at a public meeting to discuss the demolishing of an old church in order to build a new shopping centre.
   c. The story is about the local residents' fight to keep the church from being demolished.

Vocabulary 2

2 b.   4 a.   6 d.   8 d.   10 a.
3 c.   5 c.   7 b.   9 c.

Reading 2

1 The vocabulary is much richer in the original text than in the version given in Reading 1. The description in the original text is fuller and more dramatic – with many more emotionally coloured words (e.g. 'commanding attention', 'glaring', 'deprecated', 'stirring') and many more adverbs.

Some students may prefer the version in Reading 1. Like a graded reader, the language is simple and easy to understand. Other students may prefer the unsimplified version, although it is more difficult to understand, because it gives a fuller, more dramatic description of the scene.

2 a. The -*ly* words with their pronunciation and meanings are given below:

Adjectives
matronly /'meɪtrənlɪ/ fat and middle-aged (used only when talking about women)
gentlemanly /'dʒentlmənlɪ/ typical of a gentleman
ugly /'ʌglɪ/ the opposite of beautiful

Adverbs
haughtily /'hɔːtɪlɪ/ proudly and with disdain
absolutely /æbsə'luːtlɪ/ completely (used with a verb: *I absolutely agree.*, or to qualify an adjective: *It's absolutely irreplaceable.*)
forcefully /'fɔːsfəlɪ/ strongly

  b. The words used instead of 'said' are: 'announced', 'sighed', 'agreed'. They are used for variety and also to give emotional colouring and extra details to the narrative (i.e. 'announced' suggests the woman spoke loudly, clearly, and importantly; 'sighed' suggests the Chairman was tired of asking everyone to remember the formalities of a public meeting).

Unit 9 Effects of war

Vocabulary

2 c.   4 c.   6 a.   8 c.   10 a.   12 b.
3 b.   5 b.   7 b.   9 c.   11 b.

Reading and listening

3 The fact that questions and answers are separate on the printed page suggests a dialogue between an 'American' voice (the questions) and a 'Vietnamese' voice (the answers) where the two sides do not really connect.

Version B emphasizes the dialogue between the two voices. Version A emphasizes the lack of connection.

Comprehension check

1 The death of their children and the destruction (or 'napalming') of the trees.
2 It was painful for them to do so. Maybe literally, because someone with a burnt face finds it hard even to smile, and maybe just figuratively, because their suffering in the war had been so great.
3 Ornaments are only important when people are happy. When happiness ended with the start of the war, the Vietnamese stopped wearing them.
4 In the paddy fields, when they were working peacefully.
5 The bombing of the paddy fields.
6 Yes, it was sing-song speech.
7 Because the dead Vietnamese cannot talk or sing.

Points of style

1 a./c.   3 a./b.   5 a./c.
2 a./b./c.   4 b./c.

What do you think?

1 The questions are trying to find out more about Vietnamese people – 'What were they like?' as the title says. The answers talk more about the effects of war. 'Sir' is used because the 'Vietnamese' voice is being polite and humble.

2 The passive verb forms in the poem are given below:

Were they inclined . . . (line 5)
It is not remembered . . . (lines 11 and 19)
. . . the children were killed . . . (line 14)
All the bones were charred. (line 18)
. . . peaceful clouds were reflected . . . (line 22)
It was reported . . . (line 29)

Passive verbs often occur in impersonal reports, and the poet may have used them to give a distant and indirect feel to the poem. They also reinforce the idea of the Vietnamese as passive victims of war.

3 They seem like translations of Vietnamese proverbs and idioms. Much of the language in the poem has this quality of having been translated:

e.g. . . . the people of Vietnam . . . (not 'the Vietnamese') line 1
      . . . lanterns of stone . . . (not 'stone lanterns') line 2

Had they . . .? (not 'Did they have . . . ?') line 8
. . . their life/was in rice and bamboo. (not 'they spent their lives dealing with rice and bamboo') lines 20–21

4 In a very sympathetic way, as suffering human beings.

Unit 10   Story of a life

Vocabulary

2 muscular
3 recommendation
4 perceptible
5 battlements
6 resident
7 governess
8 defiance
9 charitable
10 establishment
11 abundance

Looking at plot

1 lonely/sad/unhappy
2 badly/cruelly/harshly
3 no/hardly any/only a little
4 diligent/good/hard-working
5 happy but bored/unsatisfied
6 employs . . . look after/take care of/teach
7 doesn't know/doesn't realize
8 doesn't tell
9 doesn't know/doesn't realize
10 a lot of/lots of
11 dead
12 blind and crippled

Reading

Extract 1 – Box E   Extract 3 – Box C
Extract 2 – Box 11   Extract 4 – Box 5

Comprehension check

Extract 1			
1	T	3	T
2	F	4	T

Extract 3			
9	T	11	T
10	F	12	T

Extract 2			
5	F	7	T
6	T	8	F

Extract 4			
13	F	15	T
14	T	16	T

Points of style

1 What sweet madness has seized me? (lines 1–2)
2 . . . your health (is) too sound for frenzy. (lines 3–4)
3 He groped; I arrested his wandering hand, and prisoned it in both mine. (line 8)
4 The muscular hand broke from my custody . . . (line 11)
5 I was entwined and gathered to him. (line 12)
6 The maniac bellowed . . . (line 17)
7 . . . she parted her shaggy locks from her visage . . . (line 17)
8 . . . thrusting her aside . . . (line 20)
9 . . . it is not in mortal discretion to fathom her craft. (lines 22–23)
10 . . . the lunatic sprang and grappled his throat . . . (line 27)
11 . . . on which the moon cast a hoary gleam . . . (line 30)
12 He seemed puzzled to decide what I was . . . (line 45)
13 I have again and again intimated . . . (lines 59–60)

Writing
(suggested answer)

'My God. Am I imagining things? Am I going mad?'

'You're not imagining things or going mad. You are much too sensible to imagine things, and much too healthy to go mad.'

'Where are you then? Have you only got a voice? Oh, I can't see, but if I can't feel you, my heart will stop and my head will burst. Let me touch you, whatever, whoever you are, or I won't be able to go on living.'

He felt around blindly with his hand which I picked up and held in both of mine.

'These must be your fingers!' he said, 'Your small, thin fingers. So there must be more of you!'

He pulled his strong hand away from mine. He grabbed my arm, my shoulder, my neck, my waist – he put his arms round me and pulled me towards him.

'Are you Jane? What are you? You're the right shape. You're the right size . . .'

'And I've got the right voice too,' I added. 'I'm all here – my heart too. I'm so happy to be with you again.'

'Jane Eyre! Jane Eyre!' was all he said.

Unit 11   A voice from the past

Vocabulary

2 o.	5 f.	8 m.	11 e.	14 n.
3 k.	6 c.	9 j.	12 h.	15 l.
4 d.	7 b.	10 i.	13 g.	

Reading

1 a. The narrator is a businessman and Doss is his driver.
   b. They are in a taxi.
   c. Doss has been possessed by the spirit of an old man.
   d. Doss saw an old man in the road, and managed to avoid knocking him down. Having stopped the taxi, he saw the old man get into the front seat next to him. The narrator couldn't see anything, and didn't believe Doss.
   e. Because it is about the spirit of the old man which haunts the temple.

Comprehension check

1 a. About eleven o'clock at night.
   b. No, it was deserted.
   c. To avoid hitting an old man he'd seen in the road.
   d. To examine the temple and see what had happened.
   e. They were sealed and hadn't been used for a long time, yet Doss had seen the old man coming out of them.
   f. Because he was behaving strangely and had said he'd seen something which the narrator couldn't see.
   g. Because he was being taken over by the spirit of the old man.

2 a. I had engaged a taxi for going to Kumbum, which . . . is fifty miles from Malgudi. I went there one morning and . . . in the evening . . . I . . . started back for the town. (lines 1–4)
   b. Sitting in the back seat . . . I was half lulled into a drowse. (lines 14–15)
   c. He had often brought his car for me and I liked him . . . I preferred him to any other driver whenever I had to go out on business. (lines 4–5 and line 9)
   d. It was the dark half of the month and the surrounding country was swallowed up in the night . . . hardly any light was to be seen. (lines 11–13)
   e. He was a well-behaved, obedient fellow, with a capacity to sit and wait at the wheel, which is really a rare quality in a taxi driver. He drove the car smoothly, seldom swore at passers-by . . . (lines 5–8)
   f. I was half lulled into a drowse. (line 15)
   g. I went there one morning and it was past nine in the evening when I finished my business and started back for the town. (lines 2–4)

h. He was a well-behaved, obedient fellow . . . and
exhibited perfect judgement, good sense, and
sobriety . . . (lines 5–6 and line 8)

Looking at plot preparation

1 This specific location is important because it convinces us
that the story is a true one.

2 These facts build up Doss's character. Because we know
he is dependable, we feel he is unlikely to be either drunk
or joking when he starts behaving strangely. We accept
the supernatural nature of what happens because of this.

3 These physical descriptions suggest the narrator can't
really see what is happening. At first the reader may
believe the old man exists. In this way, the writer keeps
the reader in suspense.

4 These details add to the descriptions in 3. Because the
narrator was tired and overworked, the reader can't be
sure if he should be believed. In this way more suspense is
added to the story.

Points of style

The Indian English phrases in the text are:
2 are you permitting . . .? (line 38)
3 I think we needn't care for . . . (line 47)
4 . . . engaged a taxi for going . . . (line 1)
5 . . . on the way down (lines 10–11)
6 . . . unknown fellows . . . (line 47)
7 . . . a capacity to sit . . . (line 6)

What do you think?

The ending that RK Narayan gives to the story is 3.

Unit 12   A view of Christmas

Sentence completion

The most appropriate completions are:

1 Who's that knocking on the door?
2 What are those presents lying under the tree?
3 Who is the smiling visitor with hair as white as
snow?
4 Why has he got rings on his fingers, and a red hat on
his head?
5 Why, when he sings his carol, does the white snow
fall?
6 Why does he sit by my fireside like an old friend?

7 His fingers are made of biscuits, and his tongue is
made of gingerbread.
8 Why does the world go round in front of him?
9 Why do his blue, sparkling eyes twinkle like stars?
10 See where he comes walking, out of the Christmas
scene.
11 He's dancing and singing.

Some other completions are possible, but, apart from
'gingerbread', the ones that appear later in the poem are
the most unlikely.

Comprehension check

1 The atmosphere is uneasy. The unease comes from
the description of unusual details – someone at the
window and someone at the door, the presents being
out of place, as if dropped, in the kitchen. These
suggest that something strange is going on.
The callers are the soldiers sent by Herod to kill the
children.

2 The smiling stranger, who is doing something with
the children, seems to be Father Christmas. The
description of his hair being 'white as gin', however,
makes the reader think again, and suggests that –
like an old alcoholic – he may be an unpleasant
character. Throughout the rest of the poem his real
identity becomes clearer.

3 The rubies on his fingers remind us of Herod's wealth
and power, and also of the blood on his hands.

4 The snow may be salty because someone has put salt
on it, to melt it. It may, on the other hand, be salty
with the tears of mothers crying for their dead babies.
The red colour, however, suggests that the snow is
covered in blood, which is also salty.

5 The world melting into a million suns refers to the
end of the world in a nuclear explosion.

6 The 'flame' in line 22 is the fire of hell, in which
Herod usually burns, and from which he has been
temporarily released.

Points of style

1 A raven usually caws, and the raven is a symbol of
death.

2 The spider moving to and fro suggests restlessness. It
is a powerful image, since spiders trap helpless flies in
their webs and eat them. The thread also suggests
that Herod is a puppet, like a toy spider, controlled by

a stronger evil force. The poet probably doesn't use 'like' in line 14 because the spider is not likeable. He may also be suggesting that Herod is not only similar to a spider, but that he actually becomes one.

3 fingers: holding, touching, and stroking
fuses: bombs, electricity, danger, and destruction
tongue: speaking, licking
gingerbread: a sticky child-trap, like the witch's gingerbread house in the story of *Hansel and Gretel*, something children put in their mouths

Both combinations are unpleasant.
The combination of fingers and fuses suggests it would be dangerous to let Herod hold any child.
The combination of gingerbread and tongue suggests Herod is honey-tongued and good at sweet-talking. The idea of his tongue in a child's mouth is horrible.

4 'Watch' is used in line 21 because it makes the reader think of 'Watch out!' or 'Be careful!'

What do you think?

1 The fact that the poet has set the last line apart from the others suggests that the 24 lines of the poem are for the 24th of December, or Christmas Eve. Maybe they also stand for the 24 hours of a day, suggesting that it's nearly midnight and we don't have much time left to save the world.

2 The general message of the poem is that we usually ignore the unpleasant side of the historical Christmas – the murder of the innocents by King Herod – and celebrate a sentimental, happy Christmas, where everything is good and perfect. The poet is saying that there is still evil in the world at Christmas time even now. Herod could in fact be any evil historical or present-day ruler.

13 What's in a name?

Vocabulary

1 g.	4 f.	7 a.	10 n.	13 l.
2 d.	5 j.	8 e.	11 i.	14 b.
3 m.	6 h.	9 o.	12 c.	15 k.

Reading and discussion

4 Extract A is from Act II
Extract B is from Act III
Extract C is from Act I

Plot summary

Act I

THE PLAY opens with 'Ernest' Worthing visiting his friend Algernon (Algy) Moncrieff in London. By chance Algernon discovers that 'Ernest' is really called Jack, and that he is guardian to a young woman, Cecily, who lives in his country house. Bored with the serious example he has to set Cecily, Jack has invented a fun-loving younger brother, called 'Ernest', who lives in London, and whom he often visits. In London, he explains, he is 'Ernest', and in the country, 'Jack'.

At this point Algernon's aunt, Lady Bracknell, and her daughter, Gwendolen, arrive for tea. Jack is in love with Gwendolen, and asks her to marry him. She tells him that, because of the magic of the name 'Ernest', she will accept him. Lady Bracknell says she will interview Jack before she agrees to the marriage.

During the interview Jack confesses he doesn't know who his parents were. He explains how he was found, as a baby, in a handbag at Victoria Station, by a gentleman called Thomas Cardew, who adopted him, and gave him the name 'Worthing' after the seaside town he was travelling to at the time. Lady Bracknell is not happy for her daughter to marry someone with no parents, and leaves. Although Gwendolen promises to write to him in the country, Jack is depressed at the bad news. Algernon secretly decides to visit Jack's country home, and introduce himself to Cecily.

Act II

CECILY IS in the garden of Jack Worthing's country house with Miss Prism, her governess, who is trying to get her to study. Dr Chasuble, the canon, comes to call, and Miss Prism goes off for a walk with him, leaving Cecily alone. Algernon arrives, introducing himself as Jack's brother, Ernest. Cecily confesses she has long been fascinated by stories of Ernest and invites him into the house.

Miss Prism and Dr Chasuble return from their walk, and Jack arrives from London announcing that his brother, Ernest, is dead. Almost at once, Cecily comes out of the house to say that Ernest has come to stay. Jack cannot believe the news, but when Algernon appears he realizes what has happened, and angrily tries to get Algy to leave. Algernon promises to go back to London, and Jack goes to see Dr Chasuble to make arrangements to be christened as Ernest. Algernon meets Cecily again and she confesses that, although she has never met him before, she has heard so much about 'Ernest' that she has long been in love with him. They get engaged. Algernon goes to visit Dr Chasuble to arrange to be christened as Ernest.

Gwendolen arrives unexpectedly from London, and Cecily receives her in the garden. In the course of the conversation they discover, to their great surprise, that they are both engaged to be married to Ernest. Jack returns to be confronted by the two women and Algernon enters soon afterwards. Gwendolen and Cecily refuse to forgive the two men for their deception and retire into the house.

Act III

JACK AND Algernon are forgiven when they reveal they have both made plans to be christened as Ernest that afternoon. The lovers' reconciliation is interrupted by the arrival of Lady Bracknell, who has followed Gwendolen to the country. She refuses to recognize Gwendolen's engagement to Jack, but is delighted to discover that Algernon is engaged to Cecily when she hears how rich Cecily is. Jack, however, refuses to allow the engagement between Cecily and Algernon unless Lady Bracknell agrees to his engagement to Gwendolen.

Lady Bracknell and Gwendolen are about to return to London when Dr Chasuble arrives to inform Jack and Algernon that all is ready for their christenings. When Miss Prism's name is mentioned by chance, Lady Bracknell becomes very excited and demands to meet her. Miss Prism enters and is horrified when she sees Lady Bracknell. After some discussion it becomes clear that it was Miss Prism who left Jack at Victoria Station when he was a baby, and that he is actually the eldest son of Lady Bracknell's sister, and thus Algernon's elder brother. In addition to this, Lady Bracknell remembers that he was named after his father, Ernest John Moncrieff. The play ends with the two couples in each others' arms, and, somewhat unexpectedly, with Miss Prism and Dr Chasuble also embracing.

What do you think?

Obviously the title *The Importance of Being Earnest* plays on the name Ernest. It is also ironic, since the main characters in the play are actually quite frivolous. In addition, at the end of the play Jack realizes that the lies he has told are in fact the truth, and that, although he thought he was being frivolous at the time, he has by chance been 'earnest' throughout. The subtitle *A Trivial Comedy for Serious People* suggests that, although the play is a very light-hearted comedy, it has a serious message too – that truth and fiction are often closer than we

think, and that in life dishonest behaviour is often rewarded instead of being punished.

Discussion

a. Lady Bracknell   d. Ernest (Jack)   g. Jack
b. Algernon   e. Ernest (Algernon)   h. Miss Pri
c. Gwendolen   f. Cecily   i. Dr Chasu

Project work

(a brief key to the pictures on page 73)

Lord Alfred Douglas was Wilde's lover; Constance Wilde was Wilde's wife; The Marquess of Queensbury (top left) was Lord Alfred Douglas's father; Vyvyan Holland (bottom left) was Wilde's son; *The Ballad of Reading Gaol, The Picture of Dorian Gray, De Profundis,* and *The Happy Prince* were all written by Wilde; 'Sebastian Melmoth' was the pseudonym Wilde used when travelling incognito; The Hotel d'Alsace was where Wilde died; he was buried in Paris.

Unit 15   Goodbye love

Vocabulary

1 you   4 its   7 your
2 see   5 does   8 before
3 branches   6 on which

Comprehension check

1 T
2 F (In the poem Shakespeare compares himself to autumn, dusk, and a dying fire.)
3 F (Shakespeare has noticed that his lover seems to love him more now than before, like a dying fire that burns up bright just before it goes out.)
4 T
5 T

Points of style

1 a./b.   4 a./c.
2 b./c.   5 a.
3 b./c.

What do you think?

1 It is, of course, possible that this is the case, but maybe
Shakespeare has deliberately used this unusual word
order to give a feeling of indecisiveness to the
description – as if he can't decide whether all the
leaves have already fallen or not.

2 Yes. The fact that *hang upon* is divided between lines 3
and 4 probably does have this effect.

3 No, the repeated 's' sounds in line 8 are probably there
to help suggest the soft stillness of the night.

4 Yes. The position of the words *love* /lʌv/ and *leave* /liːv/
together in line 14 suggests that Shakespeare is
probably using them as 'opposites' (i.e. 'If you love me,
you won't leave me. If you leave me, you don't love
me.'). The similarity of the sounds in both words
reinforces this.

Extract C

Unit 13 What's in a name?

LADY BRACKNELL Are your parents living?

JACK I have lost both my parents.

LADY BRACKNELL To lose one parent, Mr. Worthing, may be regarded as a misfortune; to lose both looks like carelessness. Who was your father? He was evidently a man of some wealth. Was he born in what the Radical papers call the purple of commerce, or did he rise from the ranks of the aristocracy?

JACK I am afraid I really don't know. The fact is, Lady Bracknell, I said I had lost my parents. It would be nearer the truth to say that my parents seem to have lost me . . . I don't actually know who I am by birth. I was . . . well, I was found.

LADY BRACKNELL Found?

JACK The late Mr. Thomas Cardew, an old gentleman of a very charitable and kindly disposition, found me, and gave me the name of Worthing, because he happened to have a first-class ticket for Worthing in his pocket at the time. Worthing is a place in Sussex. It is a seaside resort.

LADY BRACKNELL Where did the charitable gentleman who had a first-class ticket for this seaside resort find you?

JACK [*Gravely.*] In a hand-bag.

LADY BRACKNELL A hand-bag?

JACK [*Very seriously.*] Yes, Lady Bracknell. I was in a hand-bag – a somewhat large, black leather hand-bag, with handles to it – an ordinary hand-bag in fact.

LADY BRACKNELL In what locality did this Mr. James, or Thomas, Cardew come across this ordinary hand-bag?

JACK In the cloak-room at Victoria Station. It was given to him in mistake for his own.

LADY BRACKNELL The cloak-room at Victoria Station?

JACK Yes. The Brighton line.